holds in the body of Christ today: unforgiveness and jealousy. In his book *Total Forgiveness*, Dr. Kendall sheds light on the sin of unforgiveness and shows us how to get free from its crippling effects. In his new book *Jealousy—the Sin No One Talks About*, he explains the subtlety of this sin and how we can just pass over it thinking we could never have an issue with it. The truths in these books are vital for every Christian. These two issues must be dealt with if we are going to move on in the power of the Holy Spirit.

—RICKY SKAGGS
GRAMMY AWARD–WINNING RECORDING ARTIST

Dr. Kendall has exposed and dissected a most potent enemy of our contentment, and in doing so he has given new insight into recognizing and fighting jealousy.

—JOHN H. DIXON JR., MD
CARDIOLOGIST AND ASSOCIATE PROFESSOR
OF MEDICINE, VANDERBILT UNIVERSITY

As a professional comedian/illusionist I can tell you that the entertainment industry is a strange one; you are so often judged on how good you are compared with others. So for me, jealousy is always lurking somewhere around the corner or usually right on my back. I guess it is for all of us, so at last someone is speaking about it and how to deal with it! RT manages to unpack the whole issue so well and so clearly. Intelligent, precise, at times witty, and always insightful—I started to wish I had written it.

—JOHN ARCHER
COMEDIAN AND MAGICIAN

RT's style is to take a single topic, classify it, and explore all its ins and outs until he gets to the bottom of it. He has done it again.

—Dr. Michael Eaton
Nairobi, Kenya

How to kill jealousy and be the better for it! RT has successfully exposed both the cause and cure of arguably one of the most damaging influences in the history of the church and the world.

—Colin Dye
Senior Minister, Kensington Temple
London, England

RT hits a bull's-eye again! We neglect this message at our peril.

—Lyndon Bowring
Executive Chairman, CARE, UK

With a dynamic combination of personal disclosure, biblical depth, and Monday-morning application, RT delivers a stunning challenge in this page-turner. Vital and life changing—so buy it.

—Jeff Lucas
Author, Speaker, Broadcaster

JEALOUSY

THE SIN NO ONE
TALKS ABOUT

JEALOUSY
THE SIN NO ONE TALKS ABOUT

R. T. KENDALL

Charisma
HOUSE
A STRANG COMPANY

Jealousy—the Sin No One Talks About by R. T. Kendall
Published by Charisma House
A Strang Company
600 Rinehart Road
Lake Mary, Florida 32746
www.strangbookgroup.com

Cover design by Bill Johnson and Margarita Henry

Library of Congress Cataloging-in-Publication Data

Kendall, R. T.
  Jealousy--the sin no one talks about / R.T. Kendall.
      p. cm.
  Includes bibliographical references.
  ISBN 978-1-59979-941-4
  1. Jealousy--Religious aspects--Christianity. 2. Jealousy--Biblical teaching. I. Title.

  BV4627.J43K46 2010
  241'.3--dc22

                                        2009047403

10 11 12 13 14 — 9 8 7 6 5 4 3 2 1
Printed in the United States of America

In memory of Terry Akrill

CONTENTS

Part III
Paranoid Jealousy

Part IV
Overcoming Jealousy

FOREWORD

WHAT DO YOU think of when you hear the word *jealousy*? The spectacularly over-the-top reaction of some character in a TV soap to a frustrated romance? Your neighbor's envious scowl at the neighbor's new patio? Your colleague's snarls and mutters over a rival's promotion? It may even be that nothing much comes to mind. After all, as my friend R. T. Kendall wisely says in his title, jealousy is "the sin that no one talks about." But trust me, jealousy is big in our world, and it's more infectious, more widespread, and more subtle than we imagine. Whether it focuses on the status, lifestyle, relationship, house, or even looks of others, jealousy is all too common. In an age that puts sports personalities, film stars, and even church leaders on pedestals and labels them as celebrities and stars, it should be no surprise that many of us often find ourselves looking upward with envy. Jealousy can be triggered by an overheard phrase. You know the sort of thing: "We'll have two weeks in the Maldives next summer." "Ran that ten kilometers in under forty-five minutes." "The doctor called me at home for my advice." It can be triggered by a mere glimpse, perhaps a new car, a smart outfit, or someone sitting in the boss's office sharing confidences. It is everywhere.

So why do we overlook jealousy? There are many reasons. Perhaps we think that we are immune because we are too smart: jealousy is the sin of others. Think again. The three great Renaissance artists Michelangelo, Raphael, and Leonardo da Vinci were, notwithstanding their skill, all bitterly jealous of each other. In the sciences, the physicist Isaac Newton was a profoundly jealous man and so loathed the distinguished scientist Gottfried Leibniz that, for decades, Newton would not miss an opportunity to depict him as a liar, thief, and impostor. The great actor John Gielgud was once asked about jealousy. "I don't really know what jealousy is," he answered, before correcting himself. "Oh, yes, I do! I remember! When Larry [Lawrence] Olivier had a success as Hamlet, I wept."[1] In all probability, jealousy is not "the sin of others" but one we have slipped into. Reading this thoughtful and thought-provoking book should persuade you that no one (least of all a church leader) is immune to jealousy. Indeed, I suspect that at some time or another we are all jealous of the success or good fortune of others. If we are fortunate, the jealousy will be a passing phase; if unfortunate, it may blight the rest of our lives.

We also overlook jealousy because we consider it to be a harmless vice—something fairly minor, as if it was no more than dandruff of the soul. Yet jealousy is no harmless psychological peculiarity; if it takes root and spreads, it can become a psychological cancer that affects all we are. Consider the Christian duty to love others; jealousy renders that impossible. How about the command to praise God? Shakespeare, that wise observer of the human condition, wrote in *As You Like It*, "O, how bitter a thing it is to look into happiness through another man's eyes!"[2] Jealousy distorts everything. In French *la jalousie* means both the emotion and the window blind, and it is a fitting match; jealousy shuts out the light to our soul. The jealous find themselves blinded to both the good of others (bad) and their own blessings (worse).

Perhaps we think that we can avoid jealousy and walk away at its first appearance. Yet jealousy is subtle. Lust, greed, and hatred announce their arrival by banging on the door of our lives, but jealousy can slip in unnoticed. Like some imperceptible film of cloud creeping across the sun and slowly sapping the light of day, we barely notice it.

In alerting us to the danger of jealousy with this excellent, honest, and much-needed book, R. T. Kendall has done us all a great service. Let me commend it to you. I want to suggest it has three virtues.

First, it is surgical. RT wields a sharp scalpel and cuts through carefully to the core of the problem. There will be very few who read this book and do not reevaluate their lives as a result. Indeed, let me warn you: this book may hurt. Yet this is not a book of condemnation but of hope and forgiveness: the cuts made are those of a healer.

Second, it is scriptural. In an age where much writing is little more than recycled popular psychology with a spicing dash of biblical language, RT goes back to God's infallible Word—the Bible. The result is power and authority.

Third, it is spiritual. There are books of words and there are books of God's words: this is the latter. This is thoughtful writing by a man who has a pastor's heart, a lifetime's experience of the world, and, above all, a rich knowledge and understanding of God. This book challenges, humbles, and uplifts.

Bless you, RT, my dear friend, and to you the reader, may you be blessed too.

—J. John

PREFACE

PEOPLE OFTEN ASK me, "How long does it take to write a book?" The answer is, "It all depends." Some books take years, some months, and one (only one) took several weeks. The little booklet *The Day the World Changed* (about the terrorist attacks on September 11, 2001) was a sermon that was typed and put into print in one week.

Some books are hard to write; some are easy. Some are fun to write; some are not so fun. This one was not so fun. It was painful, since it described me more than I care to think about. It has been years in the making but took three or fourth months to write.

I have chosen to dedicate this book to a man who is possibly the most humble person I have ever met—now in heaven. I cannot thank God enough for his impact on me; I feel singularly honored to have known him. His name is Terry Akrill. Terry was a nondescript, self-effacing, and godly man whose job, until he retired, was packaging Kit Kats. He and his wife, Andrea, lived in York, England. They always attended Christians Linked Across the Nation (CLAN) gathering at St. Andrews, Scotland, which was where I met them.

Terry had the most unusual gift I have ever come across. I intend to write about it one day. And yet equally striking about Terry was his humility. He refused to be in the limelight—staying

out of sight as best as he could. The truth is, he was scared of losing his unusual gift—and consequently was extremely careful not to allow himself to have any profile in the church. As far as I could tell he was jealous of no one and certainly made sure he did not cause another to be jealous of him. He would not allow this preface to be written if he were alive, but I cherish the opportunity to dedicate this book to Terry's memory.

Working with Jevon Bolden and Deborah Moss at Charisma House is always a delight. I thank God for my friendship with Steve Strang, who has introduced me to a wider ministry in my own country. Thanks also to my close friend J. John, England's greatest living evangelist, for writing the foreword to this book. Most of all, thanks to my wife, Louise—my best friend and critic—for her patience and loving criticisms.

I write books to change lives. I pray this book will do just that.

—R. T. Kendall
www.rtkendallministries.com

COPING WITH JEALOUSY

O, beware, my lord, of jealousy; it is the green-eyed monster.[1]

—WILLIAM SHAKESPEARE

Yet he was jealous, though he did not show it, for jealousy dislikes the world to know it.[2]

—LORD BYRON

Whenever a friend succeeds, a little something in me dies.[3]

—GORE VIDAL

NOT LONG AGO I turned on our television set to watch *Meet the Press*, possibly the most important and widely watched news interview program in America, and who was being introduced to be interviewed but my old friend Richard Land. My mouth fell open. I swallowed. I looked again. I called to Louise, "Guess who is on *Meet the Press*? Richard Land." She came in and began watching.

"I will never be on *Meet the Press*," I thought to myself. On the other hand, why should I be? My views are not important; his are. But why wasn't I *excited* that Richard Land has become a national figure? I should be *rejoicing* that my old Oxonian friend Richard Land is being sought after on one of the most important news programs in the United States.

Dr. Richard Land, president of the Ethics and Religious Liberty Commission of the powerful Southern Baptist Convention, is being brought in frequently on national television programs to discuss moral issues relative to the presidential election. Richard and I were at Oxford University doing our research degrees at the same time. We were both in the same college and had the same supervisor. We became good friends. Richard's wife, Becky, used to babysit for us. And now there he was on national television. But why wasn't I thrilled to bits that my friend was now being sought after like this? I think you know.

I believe I am qualified to write this book for three reasons. First, I know what it is to cope with jealousy. My own. Second, I know what it is to cope with another's jealousy of me—both from enemies and friends. Third, I know what it is like to make other people jealous (hopefully unwittingly) and cause them to have to cope with jealousy.

It is embarrassing to admit that you are struggling with your own jealousy. I don't like to reveal that a particular person warrants my attention in that way. I can admit to other weaknesses more readily than I can my jealousy. Writing this book may have taught me more about myself than any book I have written.

Jealousy, like the Second Coming, comes in a moment when you least expect it.

For example, one evening in 1994, while we were waiting for our food to be served at a Chinese restaurant in London's Soho, Charlie Colchester, who had been churchwarden of Holy Trinity Brompton (HTB), said to Lyndon Bowring and me, "Have you guys heard about what is going on at HTB?" No, we had not. He continued, "A most unusual move of the Holy Spirit has descended on our church." He began to describe extraordinary things and then asked, "What do you make of this?" I was not blessed.

I remember the sobering day I heard this. I could take you to the very table in the restaurant where we were sitting. I recall looking at Lyndon and he looking at me. Had you put me under a lie detector and asked whether I thought what Charlie described was of God I would have said, "No." For one thing, I did not want it to be of God. The main thing, however, was that if this truly was an outpouring of the Holy Spirit—and absolutely from God—it would surely have come to Westminster Chapel first!

I looked for every reason not to believe in this, but I had a deep-seated fear this was of God.

The truth is, I was jealous.

How could God do this? I took it personally. Why would God visit HTB with an outpouring of the Holy Spirit? What had *they* done to deserve this? For example, had the clergy at HTB put themselves on the line as I had done at Westminster Chapel? How many leaders from HTB were out on the streets giving tracts to prostitutes and tourists? And why would God visit an *Anglican* church? Would God actually affirm these privileged Etonians and posh Brits with their Sloane Square accents? Who in central London had *really* borne the "heat of the day" (Matt. 20:12)? We at Westminster Chapel had, that's who.

The following Sunday I publicly cautioned all my members at Westminster Chapel that what was going on "in some places" (all knew I meant HTB) was not of God. But I was wrong. Elsewhere I have described what changed my mind (in *The Anointing: Yesterday, Today, Tomorrow* and *In Pursuit of His Glory*). Sometime later I publicly climbed down and affirmed that a true move of the Holy Spirit had fallen on Holy Trinity Brompton. That morning we prayed for their rector Sandy Millar and the people there. HTB became a sister church to Westminster Chapel. Sandy and I became very good friends. How thankful I am that God did not judge me for my jealousy and hasty comments.

We have a gracious God. He knows our frame; He does not forget that we are dust (Ps. 103:14). I might have missed entirely what God was doing—all because I was upset that God visited another church and not us.

Jealousy is an easy thing to fall into. This is because it plays into our insecurity. Like it or not, we are all insecure.

I will never forget the first time I attended a reception at

Oxford with the faculty of the divinity school and fellow research students. Here I was with Oxford dons and some of the top minds of the whole world. They had all "arrived" academically. They had the prestige and glory, the degrees, the credentials, the commendations, and books under their names. What I was not prepared for was how insecure some of them were. I had not expected this. What is more, they were insecure in the very area they should have been the most at home—their brains! But their conversations were a dead giveaway to their need for praise and admiration. One sensed a rivalry among the scholars, a defensiveness when challenged, a glee when an opposing view was put down, and an obvious delight when complimented.

There are different kinds of jealousy. The most common in the Bible is sibling rivalry—both in the immediate family and (sadly) in the family of God. There is professional jealousy—when doctors are jealous of each other, lawyers are fearful of each other's status, businesspeople are jealous of each other's success, where preachers (oh dear) are jealous of each other, and where prophetic voices even compete for who truly speaks for God! Both within and outside the church a woman may be jealous of another woman's beauty, or the best of friends can fall out over a romantic competition. There is social jealousy, when one wants to be seen at the right parties or on the social page of the newspapers. There is political jealousy, where one's rival is a threat to his or her personal influence, charm, and power. There is in some places aristocratic jealousy, where background and antiquity give a person a certain cache.

There is royal jealousy, when kings and queens claim to be the wealthiest and most respected in the world. There is national jealousy, where a country and its citizens feel superior over another. There is educational jealousy, where one boasts of the most degrees and the best schools. There is jealousy over wealth, pedigrees, job or position, talent, the size or location of one's office, background, culture, home, car, or friends.

There is, however, a benign envy (motivation for good) and a legitimate jealousy—what Paul calls a "godly jealousy" (2 Cor. 11:2). These are subjects I will look at later in this book.

But sometimes a far more vehement jealousy, sadly, is church jealousy—often found in a wicked denominational and theological rivalry among some churches. As a group of Baptists once put it, following their mission, "Well, we didn't have much of a revival last week, but thank God the Methodists didn't either." As one Kentucky preacher used to say, "Some people are jealous of your face, some are jealous of your place, some are jealous of your lace, and some are jealous of your grace."

As I said earlier, jealousy is an easy thing to fall into, but it is still an ugly thing. Jealousy frequently makes us repress—that is, we deny that we are feeling jealous. Repression means to live in denial; thus, we honestly believe what is not true because it is less painful to avoid the truth.

We happened to be in Florida during Hurricane Andrew several years ago. We were staying with close friends. With no electricity and no possibility of fishing, we had to think of things to do. So someone read aloud an article by a well-known preacher, but they did not *say* who wrote it. I said, "Wow, that is really good—who said that?" When they told me, I felt a sinking feeling in the pit of my stomach. It was a man who has opposed my theology and me. I said nothing. Then I realized how jealousy can divert you from solid *truth* merely because you don't like the person who states it. I never told anybody at the table what was going on inside me that day, but I knew I had no choice but to accept the truth of the man's statement and get over how I felt about him.

Jealousy can even camouflage as being the leadership of the Holy Spirit. I may have been on the verge of this when hearing about the move of the Spirit at Holy Trinity Brompton. Jealousy therefore sometimes comes alongside as if it were the very Holy Spirit Himself at work. Before we have had time to reflect clearly, jealousy unconsciously overrules our judgment, takes over our feelings, shapes our thinking, and masquerades as spiritual discernment. Jealousy lets us proceed and make observations as if we had the wisdom from God. When we are jealous, we tend not to see it as jealousy at all but feel a righteous disgust.

Jealousy can often be a physical feeling. We feel it in our stomachs. We can get a lump in our throats so that it is hard to swallow. For this reason, if not dealt with, jealousy can have a negative physical effect on our bodies. As holding a grudge is injurious to your health, as I pointed out in *Total Forgiveness,* so too is jealousy. Jealousy climbs inside our haughty hearts and turns our faces green while we continue to wear a plastic smile. It churns us inside while, unless we are alone, we act as though we are thrilled to bits. If we are alone, we just feel sickened but tend not to admit the real reason we feel a particular way. It can be so painful to admit you are jealous.

We are usually not jealous of those much older than we are. We are more prone to jealousy when another is much the same age as we are—or younger. Oh, yes, we are threatened by a younger person with a lot of promise, energy, good looks, and cleverness. We are normally not jealous of the heroes of a previous generation. It is safe to praise the dead. The Pharisees had no objectivity about themselves, as Jesus pointed out: "You build tombs for the prophets and decorate the graves of the righteous. And you say, 'If we had lived in the days of our forefathers, we would not have taken part with them in shedding the blood of the prophets'" (Matt. 23:29–30). The Pharisees thought they were a cut above disobedient Israelites of a previous era, not realizing how they themselves were no different. I knew of a London pastor who would not allow Dr. Martyn Lloyd-Jones's books to be sold in his church—that is, until after Dr. Lloyd-Jones died! Then it became safe to allow his books to be sold.

Those living in our own era, within the general range of our intellectual perspective or age bracket, will normally be the targets of our jealousy. Jealousy has a curious way of connecting to one's geographical location too. This is why Jesus said, "No prophet is accepted in his hometown" (Luke 4:24). The reason that a prophet is not without honor except in his own country is because we are jealous of those near us who make it "big." I happened to be in Australia when Steve Irwin, their most popular citizen and the man who made worldwide fame through his love and ability with animals, died. I was stunned to hear so many Australians criticize him. There is no doubt he was far more popular in America and Great Britain than in his own country.

I know what it is to be threatened by another person's charisma, intellect, fame, financial security, personality, charm, good looks, talent, brilliance, sense of humor, wisdom, reputation, and position. Take my friend Lyndon Bowring. He lights up a room the moment he walks into it. More people regard him as their closest friend than you can count on two hands. When he is at a table with friends, they all make eye contact with him, not me. Take Rob Parsons. I sat on the platform at a Spring Harvest celebration and watched him enthrall four thousand people with his Welsh oratory in the Big Top. I did my best to look excited. If only I could speak like that. I have watched people like J. John, Gerald Coates, Steve Chalk, Jeff Lucas, and David Pawson do the same thing—leave a crowd spellbound by their articulate flow of words, charisma, and ability to hold the attention of a vast audience. Not long ago Tony Campolo and I were speakers at a conference in Detling, Kent. His communication skills are, simply, as good as it gets. I felt utterly inferior to him.

And then there is Billy Graham. He has made more preachers jealous than you could count—not dozens, hundreds, or thousands but hundreds of thousands. I also know more church leaders who will give you their theological reasons why Billy cannot possibly have been raised up by God as a sovereign instrument of the Holy Spirit but is only a creation of the press. You can rarely get a single one of them to admit that the real issue—you could call it the elephant in the room—is not theological at all but jealousy.

I will never forget when I first met Billy Graham. I was a student at Trevecca Nazarene University in Nashville. I would not have been jealous of him at that stage; he was more of an idol. Many years later as minister of Westminster Chapel I met him again. The next day I was asked by a friend, a church leader, "What was it like to meet Billy Graham?" Before I could finish my answer, he said, "You may not agree with me, but I maintain that with a face like that he could not possibly be intelligent." Oh yes, those were his exact words. Could jealousy lie behind a comment like that?

What was often embarrassing to me was that a lot of people thought I was close to Billy Graham just because he preached for me at Westminster Chapel. "I hear Billy Graham was in London. Did he phone you?" No. Another friend told me he rode in the car with Billy Graham from Heathrow to his hotel in central London. I swallowed hard and said, "Fantastic!" Another asked, "Billy Graham is preaching at Earl's Court. Were you invited to sit on the platform?" No. As a matter of fact, when Louise and I took some Americans to Earl's Court to hear him—friends who had hoped to meet Billy through us—we were put in an overflow room to watch him on a big screen. How humbling. My friends thought I had more influence than that! Even getting close to him was out of the question.

On another occasion, I did actually sit on a platform near him at Wembley Stadium. But I noticed that other ministers there were invited to spend time with him in a private room afterward, but I wasn't. I remember the pain of going back to Victoria on the train from Wembley Park feeling left out. Had I been invited, I would not have felt jealous; but since I wasn't, I did.

Then, of course, there are those who are quick to tell you that this sort of thing—missing out on having time with Billy Graham—doesn't bother them one bit. Why then is it important for them to express this? I suspect there are basically two kinds of people: those who admit to jealousy and those who boast that they are never jealous, like those who say they could have tea with the queen of England and never tell it. I heard a pastor literally say, "I have never been jealous of anyone." I didn't know whether to laugh or cry.

Jealousy sometimes manifests as fear or resentment of another's success, speaking against the person, going on a vendetta to hurt their credibility, keeping them from being admired, or actually engaging in a conspiracy to destroy them—as in the case of King Saul pursuing David. The origin of jealousy is to be found in our natural insecurity. It is a part of our fallen nature. It is a proof of original sin, as Cain's murder of Abel shows (Gen. 4). Whereas Paul said we should "rejoice with those who rejoice; mourn with those who mourn" (Rom. 12:15), the truth is, it is often not too hard to mourn with those who mourn. Indeed, minimal grace is required to weep with those who weep. But rejoicing with those who rejoice takes considerable grace, inner security, and stature.

A true friend, therefore, is not necessarily one who will weep with you but one who will rejoice with you when you have cause for rejoicing. When you have some exciting news, your first impulse is to want to share it. But with whom? I remember telling a friend of something good that just happened to me. The expression on his face showed me that he was not thrilled—but he tried hard. I realized I should not have told him. He was a friend, yes, but hardly a good enough friend to rejoice in my good news and certainly not the kind of friend I wanted at that moment. It is lonely when you have nobody you can share good news with. But there is a lesson here—how all of us should be *slow* to share very happy news, especially if it has to do with one's self-esteem.

My friend Rob Parsons says he has a hunch that the only people we might be reasonably sure will always rejoice in our successes are our own father and mother!

Jesus rejoices in good things that come our way, and He would never knowingly make someone feel jealous.

As I wrote this last paragraph, I heard a "ping" on my computer that told me I had a new e-mail. I opened it. It contained an item that inflated my ego a bit and made me want to share it with my friends. The list narrowed down as I thought, "Whom can I share this with?" Not many. A true friend will not only rejoice when you rejoice but will also keep another from feeling jealous if you can help it.

PRODUCTIVE AND COUNTERPRODUCTIVE JEALOUSY

However, jealousy isn't all bad. There is an envy that is not sinful. Whereas jealousy that manifests as resentment is rooted in our fallen nature, there is a benign envy that is traceable to what John Calvin calls "special grace in nature." It allows for a little bit of good in all of us, that is, what is noble. This means that God the Creator gives special gifts, talents, and motivations in every human being. Special grace in nature partly means that God has instilled in all creatures—in every man and every woman—a measured potential for good. It comes through creation. Special grace in nature has nothing to do with salvation.

This concept became the foundation for the reformed doctrine of "common grace"—called that not because it is ordinary but because it is given commonly to all people. God's common grace is what keeps the world from being totally topsy-turvy. It is the reason we have law and order, policemen, firemen, doctors, and nurses. It is what accounts for the good Samaritans of this world (Luke 10) and the firemen who risked their lives in New York City on September 11, 2001. Your IQ, natural talent, personality, ability to perform, and psychological makeup are all rooted in God's common grace. It produces an

Albert Einstein, a Mother Teresa, Nobel Prize winners, a Sergei Rachmaninoff, and a Winston Churchill.

So too the good kind of envy—productive envy—is rooted in this special grace in nature. A motivation to make something of your life has its origin in common grace. God uses it to produce the movers and shakers of this world.

Therefore, one of the strangest ironies regarding envy is that it can be a positive motivation to make you do something worthwhile with your life. Martin Luther said that God uses sex to drive a man to marriage, ambition to drive a man to service, and fear to drive a man to faith. But what makes a person ambitious? The "preacher" in Ecclesiastes has the answer.

According to Ecclesiastes 4:4, "All labor and all achievement spring from man's envy of his neighbor." Really? Could this be true? If I am to believe Ecclesiastes 4:4, nothing gets done apart from envy. This envy can be either benign or evil, either productive or counterproductive. The envy described in Ecclesiastes 4:4 emerges in one of two ways (or both): (1) productive envy is the desire to outdo what has preceded you (what motivates athletes in the Olympics); (2) counterproductive envy is the wish (consciously or unconsciously) to make another feel envious, although God may overrule and turn this to good.

It is not every day that a verse leaps out at me in the normal course of my daily Bible reading plan. When this happens, I usually write the date in the margin of my Bible. On April 18, 1988, my reading included Ecclesiastes 4:4, a verse I must have read dozens of times. But for some reason this verse leaped out at me as if I had never seen it before:

> And I saw that all labor and all achievement spring from man's envy of his neighbor. This too is meaningless, a chasing after the wind.

I cannot explain why, but this verse gripped me deeply that morning. It not only took hold of me, but it also stayed with me for days and weeks and months. It would not be too much to say I was consumed with this verse for a long while. It has ultimately led to the writing of this very book. Even if the preacher (writer of Ecclesiastes) was not stating an eternal, universal principle but merely his own opinion and observation, I had a sinking feeling that verse surely described me. It should not have made me feel bad, but it did.

For one thing, I felt exposed. Embarrassed. I would not want anybody—especially my supporters or members of my church—to find out that such a verse actually described *me*. Surely I was above this. It may describe others, but not me! But if somehow it does describe me, why was I seeing this now—and not before? Was I to believe that all I have done and have achieved, such as it is, was motivated by envying what others had—or even by a desire to make people envious of me? Was it such a carnal motivation, and not the Holy Spirit, that lay behind all I have wanted to accomplish? Perhaps.

I could have told you in total honesty that I felt led of the Holy Spirit to finish the university, go to seminary, and then bring my family across the Atlantic to do research at Oxford. And I believe I was. But reading Ecclesiastes 4:4 supplied me with a parallel explanation as to why I entered and finished seminary and Oxford University. Was it the Holy Spirit, or was it explained by envy?

However, God's common grace is applied in more ways than Ecclesiastes 4:4 might allow. There are those who help others and do so without envy as a motivation. Ecclesiastes describes a lot of people but not necessarily all. But it certainly describes a lot of us. Dale Carnegie, author of *How to Win Friends and Influence People*, says that the strongest urge in a human being is the desire to feel important—or be admired. I do know that the human heart is "deceitful above all things and beyond cure. Who can understand it?" (Jer. 17:9).

My point is, there is a positive side to envy and jealousy. This book will touch on this later on, especially when it comes to God's jealousy and godly jealousy.

But the main focus will be on jealousy that is not good— counterproductive jealousy. I will deal with that jealousy that bedevils all of us in three particular ways: coping with jealousy in ourselves, coping with people who are jealous of us, and coping with the fact that we make others jealous.

I will also make suggestions as to how we all can overcome jealousy. I believe if we grasp these, it can change our lives for good—and set us free.

Jealousy is often easy to see in others but so hard to see in ourselves. And sometimes it is hard to see in others. It can also be difficult sometimes to accept that jealousy is a huge part of your hero's motivation!

Why this book? To help set you free. It should help bring us down from our pedestal. It will help us accept ourselves. It should rid us of some of our self-righteousness. It should help keep us from thinking too highly of ourselves or taking ourselves too seriously. I write books to change lives, and the purpose of writing this book is to bring us closer to recognizing and overcoming our own jealousy.

This book will help you to understand others as well as to understand yourself.

JOHN 5:44

If I can bring you to grasp John 5:44—"How can you believe if you accept praise from one another, yet make no effort to obtain the praise that comes from the only God?"—in the light of the principles laid down in this book, you will become less jealous and less desirous to make others jealous. I see this verse as one of the most important verses in Scripture and a key to coping with jealousy. Indeed, you will want to protect others from the hurt of being jealous of you. You will not be so hurt by your own jealousy. You will not take another's jealousy so seriously.

Jesus never wanted to make people jealous. The more you are like Jesus, the less you will be motivated by jealousy, the less you will be affected by others' jealousy, and the more you will grieve if you make others feel jealous. Jesus was not motivated to do what

He did because He was envious or because He wanted people to admire Him. He was totally, utterly, and absolutely jealous for the glory of God. All He ever did and said was to mirror the will of the Father: "The Son can do nothing by himself; he can do only what he sees his Father doing" (John 5:19). He is the only human being who was totally exempt from the point of view raised by Ecclesiastes 4:4.

DEFINING JEALOUSY

There are many definitions of jealousy—all of them may be apt. The complexity of jealousy allows one to define it in different ways. It has been described as the fear of another's success. It is threatened self-esteem. It is resentment toward the superior status or success of a rival or friend. It is hostility toward a rival or one believed to enjoy an advantage. It is the fear of being supplanted.

Many definitions of jealousy imply a triad composed of a jealous individual, a partner, and a third-party rival. Jealousy frequently involves three parties. Most definitions describe jealousy as a reaction to feeling threatened.

One of my first memories of being jealous was when I was ten years old. A boy I did not know came to the house next door to see my friend Dick. I resented this kid elbowing in on my territory. Dick said to me, "He gets your goat, RT. He gets your goat." That is the first time I heard this expression. His saying that to me got my goat! Although my Oxford dictionary defines this phrase as merely "to annoy," getting your goat sometimes comes close in describing jealousy.

When someone gets your goat, then chances are you are jealous—whether they try to compete for your best friend, jump the line in front of you, are very assertive and have buckets of confidence, become the center of attention, get a compliment, get chosen for a job, have a higher profile, or make the front-page news. An overly confident person often gets our goat. So does the untalented person who gets what we feel is undeserved attention. The person with very little talent but who is bubbling over with confidence will irritate us.

One of the purposes of this book is to get you to see jealousy in yourself—and admit it to yourself. We will not make progress if we sweep the dirt under the carpet.

Two Greek Words

The Greek word *zelos*—zeal, anger, boiling, or ferment—has been translated either as "envy" or "jealousy." But *zelos* can also have a positive use. *Zelos* can be good—very, very good—and it can be bad—very, very bad. Positively, it can mean "zeal" or "eagerly desiring" a spiritual gift, as in 1 Corinthians 12:31. It can refer to a "godly jealousy" (2 Cor. 11:2). *Zelos* used negatively describes a sinking feeling in your stomach when being threatened; it can arise in someone from their not excelling while seeing another excel. The Sadducees were "filled with jealousy" when they saw the successes of the earliest church (Acts 5:17; see also Acts 17:5). It is the anger that comes from your blocked goals that your rival reached. It is the agitation of not getting what you want and seeing others get what they want. It is a resentment that boils up inside when a friend or rival succeeds, surpasses us, or when we feel left out. It is the fear of being replaced. It is what we feel when being unfavorably compared to others. You can be jealous or envious of someone you have never met. You can be jealous of someone who is famous—if they are brilliant, beautiful, rich, or very happy.

There is another Greek word—*phthonos*—that means the same thing, although some modern versions are translating it as "envy." Unlike *zelos*, which can be used positively or negatively, *phthonos* in the New Testament is always used negatively except for James 4:5, referring to God's Spirit jealously yearning for us. *Phthonos* therefore can be translated either envy or jealousy, depending which version you read. The translator decides. For example, Pilate knew it was out of "envy" (*phthonos*) that the Jews handed Jesus over to him (Matt. 27:18; Mark 15:10). But some versions would use "jealous" (GNT) or "jealousy" (JB). The verbal form of *phthonos* is translated as "envying" (Gal. 5:26). Some preach Christ out of "envy" (Phil. 1:15). The two Greek words *zelos* and *phthonos* mean essentially the same thing—envy or jealousy.

ENVY AND JEALOUSY

Is there a difference, then, between envy and jealousy? Probably. Both *zelos* and *phthonos* are used in Galatians 5:20–21, translated "jealousy" and "envy." However, we are not dealing so much with the etymological meaning in the Greek language but in the way the two English words have come to be understood. Ninety percent of the time they are identical, and dictionaries use one to define the other. Envy tends to focus on the other person's *things*; jealousy includes animosity toward the *person*. We are sometimes ready to admit to envy, as when we say, "I envy your vacation—I could use one myself." But we don't admit to jealousy; it is the nastier of the two words. This is why God is not envious of us; He is not envious of our things. But He admits to being jealous of us; He wants a relationship with our person.

Envy is also coveting what others have; jealousy is the fear of losing what you have. Envy is natural and passive. Jealousy is vengeful and active. Even though I believe that jealousy is stronger than envy—or worse than envy—we should not push the distinctions too far. You can have envy and jealousy at the same time. I have chosen for the most part to refer to *jealousy* in this book, realizing nonetheless that envy and jealousy can often be used interchangeably.

Speaking generally, to oversimplify, I take the view that jealousy is stronger—and worse—than envy. This is because merely to envy basically means to covet—to want what someone else has. That exposes all of us for sure. And yet you can possibly covet without seriously hurting anybody. But that does not excuse us, because the tenth commandment says, "You shall not covet" (Exod. 20:17). We must never justify ourselves in our envy or make excuses. For the tenth commandment makes coveting—envying—a sin. As we will see below, envy was an integral part of the original sin in the Garden of Eden. The tenth commandment convinced Paul he was a sinner (Rom. 7:9). We all envy; we all sin. And yet envy is natural.

Is not jealousy natural? It certainly comes from our sinful condition, but jealousy emerges more clearly when coveting becomes resentment and the devil somehow gets in. Whereas envy is an inevitable part of our sinful condition, jealousy is envy uncontrolled. Envy—what you feel in your heart—is passive and unavoidable; jealousy—when you condone, nurse, and express what you feel—is more harmful. Envy is wanting what you don't have—but keeping the lid on. Jealousy is wanting what you don't have—and taking the lid off. We cannot avoid envy, but we must keep it from getting out of control—and manifesting in a way we will always regret.

Like it or not, then, we all have envy. We all have jealousy too. But jealousy is envy that we failed to keep under control—as when the dam bursts. The volcano erupts. The tongue becomes the fire of hell (James 3:6). Although we must confront envy in ourselves and admit to what we are feeling, jealousy is what gets us into trouble. Jealousy manifests largely as *uncontrolled resentment* and is often triggered by the fear of losing something. Whereas envy is basically coveting what belongs to someone else, jealousy wants that person to be hurt. Envy wants the person's gift; jealousy wants that person to lose their gift. Envy wants that person's beautiful new car; jealousy wants it scratched—or smashed. Envy wishes one had the other person's new home; jealousy wants it to burn down. Envy desires the person's job; jealousy wants them to get fired. Envy is coveting and therefore sin. But jealousy is a worse sin.

Jealousy is envy *manifested*. Envy is the thought; jealousy is the obsession—when you are continually preoccupied with that thought. Jealousy is what spews out the wicked comment or gives birth to the evil deed. Although it is a sin to envy, you can avoid needless trouble if you deal with it while it is *only* in your thought life. But when you allow it to govern you, dominate you, and then you *express* what you feel—whether by word or deed—you can get yourself into a lot of trouble.

You may ask: at what point does one cross over from envy to jealousy? On a scale of one to ten (one to five being envy, six to ten being jealousy), when does one cross over a line, say, from five to six? I reply: when the thought becomes an obsession. It is not always so easy to tell, but keeping this in mind, just maybe, admitting to yourself what you are really feeling could make a difference when you struggle in this area. Keep a lid on your envy. Refuse to let it grip you. Don't go there in your thoughts. Don't nurture it, don't justify it, don't dwell on it, and don't encourage it. Confess it, and turn from it.

A close friend confided in me how he feels "smug" (his word) when he hears of bad things happening to others—especially to those he doesn't particularly like, and sometimes even to people he likes. He had never admitted this to anyone before. He felt ashamed. I appreciated his honesty. It reminded me of this searching proverb: "Do not gloat when your enemy falls; when he stumbles, do not let your heart rejoice" (Prov. 24:17). It is a sin to feel smug; it is a greater sin to gloat. One way to know if you have crossed over a line into full-blown jealousy is whether you gloat if your enemy falls. The proverb continues, "The Lord will see and disapprove and turn his wrath away from him" (v. 18). Such smugness or gloating is a dead giveaway that love is absent, for love "does not envy" (1 Cor. 13:4—"love...is not jealous" [GNT]).

A great English preacher, F. B. Meyer, admitted to his struggle with jealousy when another great preacher, G. Campbell Morgan, returned to England's Westminster Chapel after being in America. "'It was easy,' he said, 'to pray for the success of Campbell Morgan when he was in America. But when he came back to England and took a church near mine it was somewhat different. The old Adam in me was inclined to jealousy, but I got my heel upon his head and whether I felt right toward my friend, I determined to act right.'"4

When we examine our hearts in this area, the procedure can be very painful. Alarming. Embarrassing. How dare we feel smug when bad things happen to others—whether friends or enemies? But we do. Our fathers called it total depravity. We in the twenty-first century tend to gloss over the raw, unvarnished, sinful condition of humankind these days. But it is this aspect of humanity that made hymn writers centuries ago use words like *vile*, *wretch*, *worm*, and *foul* in their hymns to describe all of us.

This book might therefore have an unexpected fringe benefit:

to help you to see your sin. If you are like me, having been brought up with a belief one could live without sinning if you are truly saved (a belief I no longer hold), the insights of this book could help you to see why we need to confess our sins to God every day. After all, when Jesus gave us the Lord's Prayer, the assumption was that we would *need* to pray, "Forgive us our sins, for we also forgive everyone who sins against us" (Luke 11:4). Before our lives can truly change, we need to see our sin and the need to change.

Although jealousy and envy can have their own distinct meaning, keep in mind that these words are often used interchangeably in Scripture, and I will do this too at times. Both envy and jealousy arise from the same insecurity within us. A goal for this writer, and hopefully every reader of this book, will be to keep envy—which is natural—from becoming jealousy—which may be demonic. Jealousy often means that the devil got in—and won a victory.

As we will see, God Himself is a jealous God (Exod. 20:5; 34:14). And yet it is because He loves us so much. God is jealous of every part of our lives that Satan has. It is not only because it is rightfully His, but also because He knows that when He has it all, it is how we were created to live. Indeed, "He yearns jealously over the spirit that he has made to dwell in us" (James 4:5, ESV). This shows how jealousy can be a good thing—when it is the Holy Spirit at work.

Furthermore, our own envy is an entry point in us by which God frequently gets our attention. God clearly plays into our natural desire to acquire more by giving us the promise of blessing by our giving. "'Bring the whole tithe into the storehouse, that there may be food in my house. Test me in this,' says the LORD Almighty, 'and see if I will not throw open the floodgates of heaven and pour out so much blessing that you will not have room enough for it'" (Mal. 3:10). Paul said much the same thing: "Remember this: Whoever sows sparingly will also reap sparingly, and whoever sows generously will also reap generously" (2 Cor. 9:6). In other words, God appeals to our self-interest to get our attention. Does this surprise you?

Some people might fancy that they are quite above being motivated by the promise of blessing. Just remember, the heart is deceitful (Jer. 17:9); we may think one thing and be completely wrong. The truth is, God always motivates us to obedience by the promise of our being better off if we obey.

To summarize, there are two kinds of jealousy: productive jealousy and counterproductive jealousy. Godly jealousy can be productive. There is also a benign envy that can be a motivation for doing good; God can use it. Counterproductive jealousy is what eats our souls and leaves us bitter and impoverished. It is one of Satan's favorite vehicles by which he brings us to despair and destruction.

We turn now to the main theme of this book—namely, counterproductive jealousy that is a force for evil and not for good. It comes from our sinful nature that we did not overrule by the fruit of the Holy Spirit and is evidence of a worldly, carnal spirit (1 Cor. 3:3; Gal. 5:20). James curiously calls it "wisdom"—that is, wisdom of the devil. Indeed, "bitter jealousy" is "not the wisdom that comes down from above, but is earthly, unspiritual, demonic" (James 3:14–15, ESV). The sooner we see it in ourselves and want to deal with it, the better. This book is designed to help you see it and overcome it when you discover it in yourself. It is designed to help you cope with it when others are jealous of you. It is designed to help you see when you could be causing others to feel jealous (even if inadvertently)—and how to stop it.

> Nothing in my hand I bring,
> Simply to Thy cross I cling;
> Naked, come to Thee for dress;
> Helpless, look to Thee for grace;
> Foul, I to the fountain fly;
> Wash me, Savior, or I die.[5]
>
> —AUGUSTUS TOPLADY

Part I

ORIGINAL JEALOUSY

Chapter One

SATANIC JEALOUSY

I will ascend to heaven; I will raise my throne above the stars of God.... I will make myself like the Most High.

—ISAIAH 14:13–14

When the woman saw that the fruit of the tree was good for food and pleasing to the eye, and also desirable for gaining wisdom, she took some and ate it. She also gave some to her husband, who was with her, and he ate it.

—GENESIS 3:6

But I am afraid that just as Eve was deceived by the serpent's cunning, your minds may somehow be led astray from your sincere and pure devotion to Christ.

—2 CORINTHIANS 11:3

THEOLOGIANS SPEAK OF "original sin," namely, the sin that emerged in the Garden of Eden. But this section focuses initially on original jealousy—at two levels: (1) the first sign of jealousy before God made our world, and (2) when it first manifested in our fallen world.

What we call original sin began when Satan came alongside Adam and Eve and succeeded in getting Eve to doubt God's command, "You are free to eat from any tree in the garden; but you must not eat from the tree of the knowledge of good and evil, for when you eat of it you will surely die" (Gen. 2:16–17). That command was clear enough, but the serpent said to Eve, "Did God really say, 'You must not eat from any tree in the garden'?" Eve doubted God's word, succumbed to the temptation to eat, and ate the forbidden fruit, followed by Adam (Gen. 3:1–6).

And yet behind original sin was actually original jealousy— that of Satan himself in the heavenlies before God created man. It was jealousy that lay behind Satan's decision to revolt. The prophet Isaiah was given a glimpse as to what happened. Called "morning star"—"Lucifer, son of the morning" (Isa. 14:12, KJV)—Satan fell from heaven after jealousy took over. Satan said, "I will ascend to heaven; I will raise my throne above the stars of God; I will sit enthroned on the mount of assembly, on the utmost heights of the sacred mountain. I will ascend above the tops of the clouds; I will make myself like the Most High" (Isa. 14:12–14). But the devil was brought down. Some think that this moment was described by Jesus: "I saw Satan fall like lightning from heaven" (Luke 10:18).

In a word: Satan was jealous of God. The devil apparently tried to recruit every angel in the heavens. It would seem that he succeeded with a third of them (Rev. 12:4). Peter says that God did not spare the angels that sinned but "sent them to hell, putting them into gloomy dungeons to be held for judgment" (2 Pet. 2:4). Jude added that the angels who abandoned their home "did not keep their positions of authority" and are "kept in darkness, bound with everlasting chains for judgment on the great Day" (Jude 6). Jealousy was at the bottom of it all.

This is why jealousy is so bad. It has the very breath of Satan in it. When you and I have feelings of envy, we must be extremely careful lest Satan seize the moment and exploit it to his advantage. He is the expert in this area; never underestimate his ability to put thoughts into your mind that will lead to the worst possible outcome. The devil is at home with jealousy; it is his domain. He thrives on jealousy like a vulture feeding on a dead animal. When he can tempt us with jealousy, he will.

Twisting God's command and turning Eve away from God's exact word in the Garden of Eden was Satan's first effort to seek revenge against God. He wanted vengeance for being cast down from the heavens. He has spent the whole of his time ever since trying to get men and women to follow him rather than their Creator God. "He is filled with fury, because he knows that his time is short" (Rev. 12:12). He is called the "god of this age" and "has blinded the minds of all unbelievers, so that they cannot see…the light of the knowledge of the glory of God in the face of Jesus Christ" (2 Cor. 4:4, 6).

Satanic Hate

Never underestimate how much Satan hates you. He loathes you with an icy hatred that exceeds any ire you have faced on this earth. His hatred is ultimately directed toward God. When Satan recognized Jesus as God's Son, his hate and fear compounded. On one occasion the demons cried out, "What do you want with us, Jesus of Nazareth? Have you come to destroy us? I know who you are—the Holy One of God!" (Mark 1:24). On another occasion the demons cried out to Jesus, "Have you come here to torture us before the appointed time?" (Matt. 8:29).

Satan is God's creation—never forget that. He was not created evil; he became evil. We have an enemy whose hatred of God is also directed at us. When Satan was cast down, taking with him all those who entered into his conspiracy, he devoted himself to blinding men and women. He blinds them by exploiting their hate, jealousy, and the desire for self-vindication and vengeance. All he ever does is with an attempt to defeat God. He is deceived, telling himself he will somehow win in the end. Although he knows his doom is sure, he still tries his best to take all he can with him to hell. The next time the devil, called the accuser in Revelation 12:10, reminds you of your past, remind him of his future. "And the devil, who deceived them, was thrown into the lake of burning sulfur.... [He] will be tormented day and night for ever and ever" (Rev. 20:10).

Satan may win some battles, but God has won the war.

What the devil does, then, is to tempt us. He masquerades as an angel of light (2 Cor. 11:14). He comes like a roaring lion, looking for someone to devour (1 Pet. 5:8). He does his best work through our unforgiveness. If he can get you to hold a grudge, he can play with you like a toy. Refusing to let others off the hook is your way (even if you didn't mean to) of beckoning to the devil, "Come and get me." One important advantage of totally forgiving others is that Satan "might not outwit us" (2 Cor. 2:11), so that "Satan will not outsmart us" (NLT). Therefore if he finds the seed of resentment in you, it makes easy work for him.

Unforgiveness means resentment, and resentment is at the heart of jealousy. Satan can see jealousy in us quicker than you can bat an eyelash. The moment he sees jealousy in us, he is merely waiting for the moment to exploit us, pounce on us, and engineer us to do his wish.

Don't let Satan have that pleasure with you. Don't give him that satisfaction.

My loving counsel to you: learn to recognize jealousy in yourself as soon as possible, then fear it. Fear jealousy as you would fear being trapped by a violent fire. Run from it. When you see it in yourself, do all you can to resist it.

Jealousy's Earthly Debut

When Satan came to Eve in the form of a serpent, he was making his debut on the human stage. He began by getting Eve to doubt God's words: "Did God really say, 'You must not eat from any tree in the garden'?" (Gen. 3:1). Then the devil even appealed to her love for God: "God knows that when you eat of it your eyes will be opened, and you will be like God, knowing good and evil" (v. 5). Eve caved in when she saw that the fruit was "good for food and pleasing to the eye.…She also gave some to her husband, who was with her, and he ate it" (v. 6). It was a masterstroke, a major victory for the powers of jealousy against God. Sin set in, dying set in, selfishness set in, fear set in, hate set in, jealousy set in—and with these came death (Rom. 6:23).

It was Eve's envy that led to their downfall. She saw that the fruit was good for food and "pleasant to the eye." It also was desirable for "gaining wisdom." She envied; she coveted. The original sin in the Garden of Eden is therefore traced to her doubting God's words—"Did God really say, 'You must not eat from any tree in the garden'?"—and her giving into envy. She coveted what she felt she did not have. Although you can sometimes envy without seriously hurting anybody, Eve's succumbing to envy led to Adam's sin—and that of the whole human race as well.

We should never minimize the sin of envy—and make excuses for ourselves.

"In Adam all die," said Paul (1 Cor. 15:22). "Sin entered the world through one man, and death through sin, and in this way death came to all men, because all sinned" (Rom. 5:12). That is how sin began. This is how it came to be called original sin. It is in all of us. Like it or not, we are born with it. It is traced to Satan's jealousy of God.

But could this sin not have died with Adam? After all, it is one thing for Adam himself to sin but another for the rest of us to sin as he did. Perhaps Adam's children could do a better job of it! Perhaps his offspring would have a "clean start" as it were—and be free as Adam was before the Fall. If only.

Adam and Eve passed on their fallen nature to their children. No human being has been born in this world without this fallen nature and propensity to sin.

St. Augustine posed four stages of man—from creation to his final redemption: (1) *able to sin* (when he was created—before the Fall); (2) *not able not to sin* (Adam's offspring after the Fall); (3) *able not to sin* (after conversion); (4) *unable to sin* (when we get to heaven).

"Not able not to sin," then, is the state into which all of us were born. "Surely I was sinful at birth, sinful from the time my mother conceived me" (Ps. 51:5). "Even from birth the wicked go astray; from the womb they are wayward and speak lies" (Ps. 58:3).

Although I cannot blame Satan for my own jealousy, there is a sense in which jealousy is satanic. The same rival spirit that led to Satan's downfall is mirrored in my anger when I see others exalted—and not me. I may not want to admit it, but when I am jealous of those who are successful, admired, mightily used, elevated, promoted rather than me, and more popular, I am really angry with God. After all, "It is God who judges: he brings one down, he exalts another" (Ps. 75:7). As Satan is jealous of God, I must be careful not to be like that. Otherwise I will be repeating the very sin that brought evil into the world.

The Garden of Eden was a place on the map, the fall of man a date in history. Every person who has ever lived can trace his or her ancestry and nature to the Garden of Eden and the fall of our first parents. I don't mean to be unfair, but a theology that does not take this seriously will be wishy-washy, superficial, and cause for an extremely weak Christianity.

Chapter Two

GOSPEL JEALOUSY

The LORD looked with favor on Abel and his
offering, but on Cain and his offering he did not
look with favor. So Cain was very angry, and his
face was downcast.

—GENESIS 4:4–5

I am astonished that you are so quickly deserting
the one who called you by the grace of Christ and
are turning to a different gospel—which is really no
gospel at all.... Some people... are trying to pervert
the gospel of Christ.

—GALATIANS 1:6–7

FURTHER EVIDENCE OF what happened in the Garden of
Eden was found in the offspring of Adam and Eve. Their
fallen nature was passed on to their children. Every
human being who has ever lived since the Fall in the Garden of
Eden has inherited this original sin. Eve gave birth to Cain and
then later gave birth to his brother Abel. Abel kept flocks; Cain

worked the soil. In the course of time both of them presented offerings to the Lord.

The first human account of jealousy in the Bible thus stems from sibling rivalry. It is the kind of jealousy that is described more than any other in Scripture. It is a frequent occurrence in life, when one feels less loved and appreciated than one's brother or sister. We may want to blame our parents for this; we may want to blame God.

Abel is presented by the writer of the epistle to the Hebrews as the first man of faith in human history. "By faith Abel offered God a better sacrifice than Cain did" (Heb. 11:4). Abel brought fat portions from some of the firstborn of his flock. Cain brought some of the fruits of the soil as an offering to the Lord. "The LORD looked with favor on Abel and his offering, but on Cain and his offering he did not look with favor. So Cain was very angry, and his face was downcast" (Gen. 4:4–5).

Abel did what he did by faith; he offered a sacrifice that was acceptable to God. "By faith he was commended as a righteous man, when God spoke well of his offerings" (Heb. 11:4).

Cain became jealous of his brother Abel. But it was the gospel that Cain resented. Indeed, the outline of the everlasting gospel emerges in the story of Cain and Abel. What Cain hated— namely, how Abel was given divine favor—people continue to hate. What Abel relied on—the offering from his flock—shows that we are saved by a sacrifice that takes our place; that is, our substitute. What Cain relied on—the works of his own efforts—

shows why people remain blind to the glory of Christ; that is, by trusting themselves.

THE OFFENSE OF THE CROSS

Nothing has changed from that day to this. The issue is the same: either we are saved by our own efforts or we are saved by the sacrifice of another. Cain resented that his own efforts did not satisfy God's demands. What later became known as the *offense of the cross* (Gal. 5:11) was embedded in the biblical account of Cain and Abel. To this very day people resent God's way of salvation; namely, that we are saved through the sacrifice of Jesus dying on the cross for us. People are naturally jealous that we are saved through the righteousness of Christ and not our own good works.

The historical account of Cain's jealousy of Abel is a lesson on what jealousy can lead to if not brought under control. Jealousy is capable of causing one to do extremely horrible things. Satan's jealousy of God's glory led to his revolt in heaven and sin coming into the world; Cain's jealousy of Abel led to murder. "Envy rots the bones" (Prov. 14:30).

But we may want to ask, how could Cain help but be jealous? Was it fair that God chose Abel's offering over Cain's? The obvious question is, how did Abel know to do what he did; namely, choosing an appropriate offering to God? How did he know to bring a sacrifice of blood? Was it not natural for Cain to bring an offering from his work with the soil? I can think of two possibilities as to how Abel and Cain knew what to do. First, God would have communicated His desire to them. Whatever led them to bring an offering to the Lord in the first place? Precisely how God spoke to them in those days is uncertain. Certainly God spoke by His Holy Spirit, but how this was carried out—whether by audible voice, angelic visitation, vision, or dream—I don't know.

The second possibility is that both Cain and Abel equally knew what was appropriate because they were taught by their parents. After Adam and Eve sinned in the Garden of Eden, God made garments of skin for them "and clothed them" (Gen. 3:21). This provision required the shedding of blood and constituted the beginning of the sacrificial system in the Old Testament. Their being "clothed" pointed to our need for being clothed by God's righteousness. One of the greatest hymns puts it so beautifully:

Jesus, Thy blood and righteousness
My beauty are, my glorious dress;
'Midst flaming worlds, in these arrayed,
With joy shall I lift up my head.[1]
—NIKOLAUS L. VON ZINZENDORF

God offered His grace equally to both Cain and Abel. Abel's offering was not a leap in the dark. He didn't consider it a gamble that a sacrificial offering of blood might please God. Abel did what he did because he believed God would be pleased by an animal sacrifice.

The blood of Jesus Christ, which Abel's offering prefigured, does two things: (1) it washes away our sins, and (2) it satisfies God's justice. The first is called expiation—what the blood does for us; it takes away our sin and provides forgiveness. The second is propitiation—what the blood does for God; it turns away His wrath from our sins. What Abel did is what everyone must do in order to know their sins are forgiven and that they will go to heaven when they die.

THE WORK OF OUR HANDS

What about Cain? He opted to offer the hard work of his hands. He wanted his work with the soil to atone for his sins and satisfy God's justice. Cain was determined to make his work with the soil count—which is shown by his refusal to do the right thing when he was given a second chance.

Abel's offering of a lamb prefigured atonement by substitution. This means that the lamb took Abel's place. What God required was not vegetation substituting for man but a slain animal substituting for man, or humankind. Vegetation is not an analogy to humankind, but a beast is. This is why the Law of Moses carefully unfolded the sacrificial system in terms of the slaughtering of an animal. The shedding of blood was essential. "For the life of a creature is in the blood, and I have given it to you to make atonement for yourselves on the altar; it is the blood that makes atonement for one's life" (Lev. 17:11). Moreover, in the new covenant it was not a case of vegetation substituting for sinful man or even beasts substituting for sinful man. Instead, *God became man* and was the perfect man substituting for sinful man. When God Himself became man, He who knew no sin was "made sin" for us, "so that in him we might become the righteousness of God" (2 Cor. 5:21).

Put simply: Cain sadly did not want to accept God's prescribed method of worship. He preferred to bring the labors of his own hands. He tried to appease his conscience by good works. Whereas the great hymn "Rock of Ages" by Augustus Toplady says, "Nothing in my hand I bring, simply to the cross I cling," Cain was saying, as it were, "In my hand a price I bring, simply to *my works* I cling."

There is much, much more to this story than sibling rivalry. The heart of the gospel is at stake. A love for the gospel and a hatred of the gospel crosses family, culture, education, race, and natural prejudices. It is often true that "blood is thicker than water," meaning that families and blood relationships tend to stick together. But there is one thing that transcends this—the gospel. The gospel not only gives the believer a new family; it will divide families. Jesus said, "A man's enemies will be the members of his own household" (Matt. 10:36). You cannot make a person—whether your closest relative or dearest friend—love the good news that we are saved by Jesus's death on the cross. What thrills one infuriates another—and it transcends one's background and biases. "That day Herod and Pilate became friends—before this they had been enemies" (Luke 23:12). A hatred of Jesus was sufficient to bring two enemies together.

The most offensive thing about the gospel of Jesus Christ

is the claim that we can only be saved through Jesus—who is God's one and only Son—and by His death on the cross.

Have you ever wondered why the Quran teaches that Jesus did not die on the cross? This way they avoid Christ's atonement. Islam not only does not believe that Jesus is the Son of God (but only a prophet) or that He was not raised from the dead, but they also do not even believe He *died* on the cross in the first place.

Canon Andrew White, who was the archbishop of Canterbury's envoy to the Middle East, introduced me to the late Yasser Arafat—with whom I developed a warm and fairly close relationship. I stressed one thing to Arafat: that Jesus *died*. President Arafat wanted to say that Jesus ascended to heaven. "Yes, that is true," I said, "but He *died* first, was raised from the dead, and *then* ascended to heaven." Islamic teaching bypasses not only Jesus's substitutionary atonement but also His very death! It is because the real offense of Christianity is that we are saved through Jesus's blood. Islamic teaching avers that Jesus did not shed a drop of blood on the cross but was delivered from the cross by Allah.

I have wondered how long it would be before various cults would line up with Islam. Since I began writing this very chapter, I flew to Boise, Idaho, where there is a large population of Mormons. While I was there, a front-page article in the *Idaho Statesman* reported that Islamic and Mormon leaders were now talking together because they found out how much they had in common. "U.S. Muslims, Mormons Forge Unique Bond," said the headline on April 2, 2008.[2] This is but the beginning. You can expect more of this sort of thing because all who oppose salvation by the blood of Jesus will cross cultural, racial, theological, and family ties and eventually stand together.

The way Cain felt about Abel is the way all false religions feel about the God of the Bible—New Age, cults, Buddhism, Hinduism, and Islam. People naturally resent the God of glory who is revealed in Scripture. They resent that people who come to Jesus Christ would turn away from natural religion and honor the God revealed in the Bible. "How dare this God demand such worship" is a typical reaction of humankind to the true God. The resentment springs from jealousy; people naturally want the god they are comfortable with to be the true God. It is ultimately jealousy toward true believers that is at the bottom of one's hatred of Jesus and God's way of salvation. People who reject the gospel hate God's way of being pacified through the sacrifice of Jesus, and this hostility spills over into jealousy toward those who claim to be saved through Jesus alone. "If the world hates you," said Jesus, "keep in mind that it hated me first" (John 15:18).

Cain's jealousy of Abel, then, foreshadowed the offense of the cross and the way people naturally feel about God's way of salvation.

Cain had equal opportunity to do as his brother did. Cain was given a second chance. "Then the LORD said to Cain, 'Why are you angry? Why is your face downcast? If you do what is right, will you not be accepted? But if you do not do what is right, sin is crouching at your door; it desires to have you, but you must master it'" (Gen. 4:6–7). Therefore, before God rejected Cain entirely, He gave him a second warning. It was obvious that what God required of Cain and Abel was precisely what Abel had brought. So God in effect said to Cain, "If you do the same thing, you too will be accepted." We therefore say to any Muslim, Mormon, or Hindu, "If you will turn from your good works and trust what Jesus did on the cross, you too will be saved."

THE CRAZY THINGS JEALOUSY MAKES US DO

Jealousy is so strong that, if not resisted, it will prevent us from sane, clear, reasonable thinking. Rather than admit we are wrong and someone else is right, we will often stick to our guns—we cannot bear losing face. Cain did not want to believe that his brother Abel got it right.

It is not necessarily a sin merely to have a feeling of jealousy. We have seen that there is such a thing as productive jealousy. God can use it.

But this book is largely about counterproductive jealousy, and that is what was going on with Cain. And yet a feeling of jealousy could be *temptation* to jealousy, not necessarily sin— yet. Although jealousy is a work of the flesh, by which we come to naturally, it is not committing sin unless you give in to the feeling. Jealousy becomes a sin when given in to. "If you do not do what is right, sin is crouching at your door" (Gen. 4:7). An act of the will is required—whether to give in to jealousy or to resist it.

Jealousy therefore can often be like temptation. It is not a sin to be tempted. There is a difference between temptation and sin. One can have feelings of jealousy, but these feelings must be recognized, refused, and resisted. Remember the three Rs of spiritual warfare: recognize, refuse, resist. One can be wrongly sexually aroused, but such feelings must be recognized, refused, and resisted. "Each one is tempted when, by his own evil desire, he is dragged away and enticed. Then, after desire has conceived, it gives birth to sin; and sin, when it is full-grown, gives birth to death" (James 1:14–15). So with jealousy; when one has such feelings and they are not resisted, they give birth to sin; and when it is full-grown, it gives birth to death. That is what happened with Cain.

"Cain attacked his brother Abel and killed him" (Gen. 4:8). Full-grown jealousy gave birth to death.

Cain's hatred of Abel, ironically, was not ultimately directed toward Abel—but God. Abel had no righteousness in himself. Abel was not claiming to be good. It was his offering of the firstborn of his flock that pleased God. And yet Cain took it out on Abel. When the world is angry with us, they are really angry with God. One of the first rules of dealing with persecution is not to take persecution personally. It is God, not you, whom they hate. After all, we are not claiming any righteousness in ourselves whatever! We are only pointing to Jesus Christ as our way of being saved. And the same gospel is for all.

In precisely the same way, then, that Cain was given an opportunity to do what Abel did, so do we say to those who persecute us, "You can trust Jesus just as I did. He died for you as well as for me. You too can be saved."

But if jealousy sets in, it becomes very difficult to overcome. When the problem is jealousy, the possibility of peace becomes extremely difficult.

Cain could not cope with the fact that Abel got it right and that he got it wrong. Pride set in. Where there is jealousy, there is an injured ego. All Cain had to do was to say, "Thank You, God. I want to please You with an acceptable offering." But no. He was jealous that Abel got it right first and could not bring himself to affirm Abel by doing what Abel did.

Jealousy can lead us to do crazy things, like losing one's own soul. That is what Cain did. Cain became a prototype of those who are reprobate, or apostate, as opposed to God's elect, or saved. Yet this should also help us to see once and for all that those who are damned are condemned by their own sins, and those who are justified are saved by a righteousness outside themselves. The one who is justified can take no credit for it; the one who is damned can only blame himself or herself.

I have known of those who have said, "If so-and-so is going to be in heaven, I want to go to hell. I don't want to spend any time in heaven with that person." Isn't that extraordinary? That is what jealousy, if not brought under control, can lead to.

"It desires to have you, but you must master it" (Gen. 4:7).

How do you master it? Swallow your pride. Get over it! Don't be a fool. Don't be destroyed. Don't go to hell! Recognize that God is not looking to the works of your hands; He wants you to come through His Son, who died for your sins. Don't trust your works, even the best of them.

When you give in to jealousy, you allow Satan to become himself in you. When you manifest the fruit of the Holy Spirit, it is because you allow Jesus to become Himself in you. The result will be "love, joy, peace, patience, kindness, goodness, faithfulness, gentleness and self-control" (Gal. 5:22–23). When you allow Satan to become himself in you, you will eventually manifest "sexual immorality, impurity and debauchery; idolatry and witchcraft; hatred, discord, jealousy, fits of rage, selfish ambition, dissensions, factions and envy; drunkenness, orgies and the like" (vv. 19–21).

Abel's offering was carried out "by faith," says Hebrews 11:4. He was moreover commended as "a righteous man, when God spoke well of his offerings." This simply means that God imputed, or credited, Abel with righteousness (Rom. 4:5). God saw Abel as though he were righteous. That is the way God sees you and me—as righteous, all because we are trusting in the sacrifice of Jesus who shed His blood for us.

But sadly this often makes people jealous, even though they can equally have the same exact salvation.

Did Abel know that he was regarded as righteous? Yes, he did. He had the greatest witness of all: *God* testified of his gifts; God "spoke well of his offerings" (Heb. 11:4). This goes to show we can *know* where we stand with God! It is not a vain claim or prideful affirmation to say you know you are saved. All you are doing is claiming the righteousness of another!

> My hope is built on nothing less
> Than Jesus' blood and righteousness;
> I dare not trust the sweetest frame,
> But wholly lean on Jesus' Name.[3]
>
> —EDWARD MOTE

Original jealousy was jealousy of God. That is what brought Satan's downfall; it is what brought Cain's downfall. When people are jealous of the people of God, it is ultimately directed toward God Himself.

We must therefore learn not to take their jealousy of us personally. It is God they hate, not us.

But their jealousy may still result in our demise, as it did with Abel. There will be those who intend to destroy us—and succeed. They may take our lives, and they may try to ruin our reputations. As Martin Luther wrote, "And though they take our life, / Goods, honor, children, wife, / Yet is their profit small."[4] Among Jesus's last words was His command for us to go into all the world to preach the gospel—and make disciples (Matt. 28:19). Arthur Blessitt observed that Jesus said, "Go," adding, "But He didn't say you would come back!" But we are in good company. "If the world hates you, keep in mind that it hated me first" (John 15:18).

We may be hated by those who are jealous of us because in fact we got it right. And yet the fact that we got it right regarding the righteousness of Jesus is owing to the sheer grace of God. We have the Holy Spirit to thank. "No one can come to me," said Jesus, "unless the Father who sent me draws him" (John 6:44). "The Spirit gives life; the flesh counts for nothing" (v. 63). We claim no merit in ourselves because we got it right; faith is a gift of the Holy Spirit. We love God because He first loved us (1 John 4:19). Therefore we do not expect God to thank us. As Jesus said, "So you also, when you have done everything you were told to do, should say, 'We are unworthy servants; we have only done our duty'" (Luke 17:10).

Finally, there will be no gloating on that final day. We will simply rejoice in the vindication of our Lord Jesus Christ. "Therefore God exalted him to the highest place and gave him the name that is above every name, that at the name of Jesus every knee should bow, in heaven and on earth and under the earth, and every tongue confess that Jesus Christ is Lord, to the glory of God the Father" (Phil. 2:9–11).

The difference between a Christian and non-Christian is that the Christian confesses Jesus as Lord now. Everybody will do it then.

Chapter Three

RACIAL AND NATIONAL JEALOUSY

I will make you into a great nation.

—Genesis 12:2

When [Hagar] knew she was pregnant, she began to despise her mistress [Sarah].... "You shall name him Ishmael.... He will be a wild donkey of a man; his hand will be against everyone and everyone's hand against him, and he will live in hostility toward all his brothers.... I will make him into a great nation."

—Genesis 16:4, 11–12; 21:18

Two nations are in your womb, and two peoples from within you will be separated; one people will be stronger than the other, and the older will serve the younger.

—Genesis 25:23

I GREW UP IN Kentucky when there were but forty-eight states (before Hawaii and Alaska were brought in). We had a slogan in those days—"Thank God for Arkansas." This was because Kentucky was *forty-seventh* in educational standards. Arkansas (thankfully) was forty-eighth. Had it not been for Arkansas, then Kentucky would have been at the bottom, thus making our reputation even worse as the state with so many uneducated people. "Thank God for Arkansas."

So in Kentucky we had Arkansas jokes. In Indiana they have Kentucky jokes. In Texas they have Oklahoma jokes. In Ireland they have English jokes—"An Englishman thinks that manual labor is a Spanish musician." In England they have Irish jokes and French jokes. In France they have German jokes. In Germany they have Polish jokes. In Poland they have Russian jokes. The jokes are all the same—poking fun at their rival nation's presumed lack of intelligence.

I am not able to find in Scripture when a national rivalry or racism first emerged. National rivalry may have come first; racial issues may have come later. It is not unlikely that there were rivalries between tribes and nations from very early on in those clans described in Genesis 10. It is also not unlikely that there was an incipient racism—even if it had nothing to do with the color of one's skin—from earliest times. For racism has its origin in the human heart, not in facial features, the shape of one's body, or the color of their skin. We all find it difficult to live side by side a long time with the same people; it is only a matter of a few days that something about someone will irk us. My grandpa McCurley, who was Irish, whom we visited every summer in Illinois for two weeks, used to say as we were leaving, "Glad to see you come; glad to see you go." As they say of the best of company, "They are like fish; after three days they begin to stink."

The problem is, what irritates us about people will find its way into facial features, geographical origins, accents, and mannerisms. We will connect it to their background in some way. We will somehow find a way to vent our frustrations by insulting them or putting them down one way or another. When we enjoy them, they are the Smiths, the Joneses, the Whites, the lovely neighbors. But when we start disliking them, they suddenly become "Americans," "Brits," or "Poles."

There was a time in human history when all tribes and nations in the whole world spoke the same language. This unity of language will return when we get to heaven. (All will speak English with a Kentucky accent!) The origin of nations with separate languages came when God scattered the people throughout the earth for building the Tower of Babel. He confused the language of the whole world (Gen. 11:1–9).

ISAAC VS. ISHMAEL

When God promised that He would make Abraham into a "great nation," in one stroke He allowed for the possibility of jealousy to emerge. Abraham no doubt was pleased with this promise; bystanders who were not of the seed of Abraham would feel differently. The predictable reaction of the people of the seed of Abraham to the news they would be a great nation: "Fantastic! Wow! We are a chosen people." But the reaction of those *people outside* of Abraham's seed: "*Hmmm*. Not so sure we like that." Enter jealousy.

Abraham had two sons: Ishmael (born of Hagar) and Isaac (born of Sarah). The whole of the Arab world are descendants of Ishmael. Had Abraham waited for God to keep His word without Abraham's manipulation, there would have been only one son—Isaac. But Abraham began to doubt God's word and felt he needed to help things along. At Sarah's suggestion he slept with Hagar, Sarah's maidservant, and Ishmael was born. This was the beginning of the greatest, ugliest, and most dangerous national and racial rivalry the world has ever known—so painfully relevant at the present time.

The problem in the Middle East today is explained by jealousy—the sin no one talks about.

The whole thing was Sarah's idea. But once Hagar became pregnant, everything went wrong. Hagar and Sarah turned against each other—Abraham was caught in between. God gave Hagar a promise that she should not run away from Sarah and Abraham, that she would have a son—to be called Ishmael. Things were never to be the same again.

Abraham had regarded Ishmael as *the* promised child. He had no complaints; Ishmael met the criterion.

But one day God said, "Wrong, Abraham. Sarah will conceive; Isaac is coming." This did not bless Abraham. "If only Ishmael might live under your blessing!" he pleaded (Gen. 17:18). The eventual result was that Abraham had to do one of the most difficult things of his life. After Isaac was born, Sarah had further advice for her husband: "Get rid of that slave woman and her son." God endorsed Sarah's word this time: "Listen to whatever Sarah tells you, because it is through Isaac that your offspring will be reckoned." But there was more: a promise concerning Ishmael, namely, that he too would become a nation (Gen. 21:10–13). So Abraham said good-bye to Ishmael. Abraham would not see Ishmael again—or his seed, but the rest of the world eventually would.

When I first conceived of writing this book I had not realized how much the subject of jealousy in the Bible would be connected to sibling rivalry. Nancy Samalin said, "Sibling rivalry is inevitable. The only sure way to avoid it is to have one child."[1]

And yet the rivalry between Ishmael and Isaac was not personally with each other but with their mothers and then their offspring in future generations. Furthermore, the racism that has been so volatile between the descendants of Ishmael and Isaac has nothing to do with the color of their skin. It is—at least for some of us—often difficult to tell the difference between a Jew and an Arab. The same is true of Indians and Pakistanis, the Polish and the Russians. But rivalries between these peoples exist. Racism in America today exists not merely as an issue with whites and blacks but with Hispanics and many other ethnic groups.

Almost all national rivalry can be traced to jealousy. And

with whom does the buck stop? Like it or not, it stops with God. It was He who promised to make Abraham into a great nation. It was He who said to Rebekah, the mother of Jacob and Esau: "Two nations are in your womb" (Gen. 25:23). Indeed, with *every single one of us*, "He determined the times set for them and the exact places where they should live" (Acts 17:26). This is why our jealousy is, at bottom, always anger toward God. And yet, as we will see later, it is *knowing* this that gives us a way forward as to how to overcome jealousy. When I come to terms that my problem with jealousy is really with God—and not people—I can cut through my feelings and focus on the true solution, namely, to get right with Him.

SIBLING RIVALRY

Parents cannot stop sibling rivalry, but they should do all they can to prevent it. For example, parents do their children no favor to show favoritism. It is unfair to the rest of the children; it is equally unfair to the one who is smothered with special attention. It often turns the favored one into being a "spoiled brat," like Jacob's son Joseph, making him or her unpopular with their siblings as well as with everybody else. People like this often grow up never knowing why they put people off, sometimes making their friends jealous and not being very liked by their peers.

I think Abraham may have been a good dad. He gives every indication of being a caring father. But his son Isaac and grandson Jacob were far from perfect parents. And yet I find this encouraging. When I recall that Isaac was God's promised child, that Jacob was loved by God (Mal. 1:2), and that David, Israel's greatest king, was a man after God's own heart (1 Sam. 13:14)—and that these men were arguably among the worst parents in biblical history—it shows how God uses imperfect parents.

Isaac and Rebekah were equally guilty as parents in playing favorites. Isaac was partial to Esau; Rebekah showered her affection on Jacob. Isaac and Rebekah had waited twenty years for their children to come along. Rebekah had been barren, and Isaac prayed to the Lord on her behalf. The Lord answered—doubly. When she became pregnant, there were twins in her womb. The Lord said to her, "Two nations are in your womb...and the older will serve the younger" (Gen. 25:23). Esau was the oldest, by a few moments, and it could be that Rebekah was biased against Esau and toward Jacob from the start—owing to this prophetic word. This is speculative, of course, but one cannot but wonder if this prophetic word to Rebekah caused her to feel as she did. If so, she may have wanted to blame God for the way she felt. In any case, one could appreciate that Rebekah was predisposed to prefer Jacob in the light of that word before the twins were born.

In any case, these twins would demonstrate a jealousy that prefigured the two nations they would become. The rivalry between Israel and Edom in years to come began with these two boys as they grew up. All national rivalries and racial tensions have their origin in the way we were shaped as children.

However, as far as one can tell, there was no parental influence in the matter of Esau selling his birthright to Jacob. Esau grew up loving hunting; Jacob was what I would call a "mama's boy"—quiet and "staying among the tents" (Gen. 25:27). Often children like these will be opposites. If the first child is scholarly, say, the second will excel in sports; if the first is serious, the second will be more sanguine. There is an instinct to be different and to outdo one another, choosing ways to do this that come fairly easily.

Jacob was jealous of Esau because Esau was the older child, hence the firstborn. Being the firstborn in ancient times meant double the inheritance. This, of course, was out of both Esau's and Jacob's hands, but situations like these don't stop jealous feelings. We will be jealous over the way God made those close to us—their good looks, intellect, pedigree, personality, ability in sports or hobby. You can be sure that Jacob grew up keenly aware he was destined to be number two in the scheme of things. But even his name—Jacob ("he grasps the heel," meaning he was a supplanter or deceiver)—suggests that he was a shrewd manipulator. In ancient times an individual's name often denoted his or her character and life's calling.

One day Esau came in from hunting, extremely hungry. He ordered Jacob, "Quick, let me have some of that red stew! I'm famished!" Jacob seized the moment. Whether he had been waiting for this for a good while, who knows? We only know that Jacob replied, "First sell me your birthright." It was a weak moment for Esau. He reasoned that he was about to die anyway and rationalized, "What good is the birthright to me?" (Gen. 25:30–32). It was faulty, foolish, and fatal thinking. The writer of Hebrews called Esau "godless" who "for a single meal sold his inheritance rights as the oldest son" (Heb. 12:16).

Jacob refused to accommodate his brother until Esau swore an *oath* to him. "Swear to me first," said Jacob (Gen. 25:33), knowing that this totally guaranteed that Jacob would—from that moment—have the rights of the firstborn. There were two ways you told the truth in ancient times—either by promise or by swearing an oath. Both were supposed to be truthful and reliable, but only the oath "put an end to all argument," as the writer of Hebrews put it (Heb. 6:16). Your mere word, or promise, may or may not be reliable; but if you swore an *oath*, you absolutely told the truth and kept your word. So Esau actually swore an oath to Jacob, selling his birthright. This was irrevocably turning over his full rights as the firstborn to Jacob. Then—and only then—did Jacob give Esau some bread and some lentil stew (Gen. 25:33–34).

You can be sure that the jealousy that existed between the two brothers was compounded from then on. Sadly there was little love between them.

But there was more. At the time Isaac was ready to give his patriarchal blessing to his two sons, Rebekah engineered a further deal: to get Jacob to steal their father's blessing from Isaac. The patriarchal blessing had a prophetic significance; it was like an oracle from God Himself. It was the same as the oath—unchangeable, trustworthy, and final. What the patriarch declared, went. To get the patriarchal blessing was therefore to secure not only the patriarch's blessing but also *God's* blessing. Rebekah so wanted Jacob, not Esau, to get this, but Isaac intended to give it to Esau. Jacob disguised himself before the aged, blind patriarch, and Isaac unknowingly bestowed his blessing on Jacob, thinking the whole time he was giving it to Esau. When Isaac realized what had happened, it was too late. He had blessed Jacob and "indeed he will be blessed!" declared Isaac (Gen. 27:33). It was this statement that gave Isaac a place in the great faith chapter of the Bible—Hebrews 11. By sticking to his guns, going against his wish for Esau but respecting the oath, "By faith Isaac blessed Jacob and Esau in regard to their future" (Heb. 11:20). Esau got a blessing from Isaac, but it was miniscule compared to the blessing given to Jacob (Gen. 27:27–40).

It was a pitiful scene. Esau cried out to his father, "'Do you have only one blessing, my father? Bless me too, my father!' Then Esau wept aloud" (Gen. 27:38). The writer of Hebrews said that Esau "could bring about no change of mind, though he sought the blessing with tears" (Heb. 12:17).

The jealousy that Esau now felt toward his brother became all the more intense. "Esau held a grudge against Jacob because of the blessing his father had given him" (Gen. 27:41). He promised himself that he would kill his brother Jacob. It led to Jacob leaving the area entirely. Jacob spent years in fear of Esau. He did not meet up with his brother for a long time. Even though it turned out to be a friendly meeting when they finally met,

Jacob never really trusted Esau and turned down an opportunity to be near his brother (Gen. 33:17).

JEALOUSY CAN LEAD YOU TO THE GREATEST GOD-MOMENT IN YOUR LIFE

Jealousy is an awful sin. It divides, engenders fear, causes one to be preoccupied with a single person, is bent on vengeance, will become the center of one's thoughts and conversations, is a vehicle for the devil to keep one from joy, is the opposite of love, and can be an opening for the demonic to take hold of one's being and personality. And when it takes place between brothers, it is all the sadder. As we saw, Cain killed Abel over jealousy, and Esau would have destroyed his brother at one stage. And, who knows? Perhaps Jacob was right in staying away from Esau toward the end of his life. The price Jacob paid for manipulating Esau's birthright and stealing Isaac's blessing was enormous, even if it carried with it the blessing of God.

It is an axiom I preach: the greater the suffering, the greater the anointing; the greater the anointing, the greater the suffering. Nobody was blessed in the Old Testament more than Jacob—whose name was changed to Israel. But nobody suffered more than Jacob. That suffering consisted in part in the fear of Esau's jealousy—which Jacob had a lot to do with.

And yet God was in some sense at the bottom of it all; He foresaw it, allowed it, and did so for His own inscrutable purpose. "Jacob I loved, but Esau I hated" (Rom. 9:13). Some Greek scholars point out that "hated" means "loved less." I don't want to be insensitive, but like it or not, that is the way it is. God permitted the whole scenario as His plan and purpose. Why? You tell me. I pass the buck to Jesus; He passed the buck to His Father: "I praise you, Father, Lord of heaven and earth, because you have hidden these things from the wise and learned, and revealed them to little children. Yes, Father, for this was your good pleasure" (Matt. 11:25–26).

Take comfort from this: if people are jealous of you, it falls within God's purpose for you. If you suffer from sibling rivalry, you aren't the first! And if you are the one who is jealous, learn from Esau's folly; he made an irrevocable choice. And if you are running from jealousy like Jacob, ask yourself whether you may have caused it. God may be allowing it, yes, but do you want the responsibility on your hands so that you live in fear as Jacob did? God is sovereign, but Jacob was responsible nonetheless for all he did—and he suffered the consequences of it.

And yet the whole thing drew Jacob close to God. Have you heard of Jacob wrestling with God (Gen. 32:22–26)? Do you know what was going on then? Do you know it is what led to his being named Israel (vv. 27–28)? And did you know that the entire episode took place because Jacob was scared to death that Esau was closing in on him (vv. 1–21)?

In other words, Jacob's fear of Esau's jealousy led him to the greatest experience with God he ever had!

Perhaps the jealousy you are coping with will do that too. I pray it will. When God is at the bottom of something, something good will come out of it. It did with Jacob. Jealousy became a tool to bring Jacob face-to-face with God. He actually put it that way: "I saw God face to face" (Gen. 32:30). I do not believe this was literal since no person has seen God (John 1:18), but the *sense of God* was so real that it was as though he saw Him face-to-face. God may be pleased to do that with you too—all because you were coping with someone's jealousy of you.

Paul even reckoned that the salvation of Gentiles might make Israel envious, or jealous. Being an apostle to the Gentiles Paul hoped to arouse his own people "to envy and save some of them" (Rom. 11:14). In other words, Paul hoped that there would be such success with the gospel offered to and received by Gentiles that it would make Israel realize what they missed—and come to Christ. It did not happen, but it still might happen yet! I pray for the lifting of the blindness on Israel—that it might come any day! Whether envy will have anything to do with it, who knows?

And yet all this coping with jealousy and insecurity of Jacob was to have huge influence outside his family. Generations later would reap what was sown in the sons of Esau and Jacob. Esau became Edom—a nation that was to be a thorn in Israel's flesh for a long time. In other words, a family squabble turned into wars between nations down the road. All racial and national rivalries have their origin in the human heart—which is desperately wicked (Jer. 17:9, KJV). We never know what our jealousy will lead to.

The art of diplomacy in race relations, national rivalries, and international tact will always be connected to one's sensitivity to a leader's fragile ego, jealous feelings, and sense of insecurity. World War III could be precipitated by the slightest unguarded comment to or by a national leader. The best of men are men at best, and none of them had perfect parents.

Part II

HOW GOD USES JEALOUSY
TO PREPARE US

Chapter Four

MOTIVATIONAL JEALOUSY

Leah had weak eyes, but Rachel was lovely in form, and beautiful.... And he [Jacob] loved Rachel more than Leah.... When the LORD saw that Leah was not loved, he opened her womb, but Rachel was barren.... When Rachel saw that she was not bearing Jacob any children, she became jealous of her sister. So she said to Jacob, "Give me children, or I'll die!"

—GENESIS 29:17, 30–31; 30:1

God moves in a mysterious way His wonders to perform.[1]

—WILLIAM COWPER

THEIR JEALOUSY, OUR preparation. That is the underlying theme for this section of my book. In a word: see their jealousy of you as God's way to get your attention and prepare you for what lies ahead. Their jealousy is a way of refining and increasing God's anointing on you.

I have wanted a greater anointing on my life and ministry

more than anything. Sometimes I think I want it *too* much. I am not sure whether it is a spiritual or natural desire. All I know is, I would do *anything* for an increased anointing of the Holy Spirit on me.

And yet I have learned one thing about this in the last thirty years or more. God's way of increasing and refining my anointing has not been the way I had hoped He would do it. I wanted it to come from prayer—my prayer life and from others laying hands on me. And perhaps it has. I am sure this has had some benefits. But all I know is, the chief phenomenon that has been pervasive in my life over these years has been the way I have been driven to my knees to seek God's face and to practice what I preach, especially regarding total forgiveness.

I wish I could tell you that I have been persecuted by the world. I wish I could give reports that, as a result of our Pilot Light ministry (going to the streets of Westminster and around Victoria in London), I had been threatened by non-Christians, the police, and the government. No. And yet the Pilot Light ministry had brought persecution—from Christians! What we had to do at Westminster Chapel irked so many people. You will ask: Were some of those people jealous of us? Yes. Those were not bad people; they believed they were governed by a godly jealousy. They thought they were losing their beloved Westminster Chapel and I was taking it away from them. They feared they were losing the chapel they always knew and loved. They didn't like it that we had altered traditions (singing contemporary hymns and giving an altar call) and brought in ways to do things that they hoped would fail—but they didn't fail. What is more, their criticisms shaped me as a person, and the result has been more insight into the Word of God than I have ever known.

Jealousy can be a very useful motivation. Jealousy is often used of God to prepare us for our future as much as anything in the world. He gets our attention by His own jealousy. He uses "their" jealousy—friends, relatives, and enemies; He uses *my* jealousy. Their jealousy of me can drive me to my knees—to bring me closer to God. Funnily enough, my jealousy of them can also drive me to my knees—to bring me closer to God. When William Cowper wrote the magnificent and profound hymn, "God Moves in a Mysterious Way," I don't know if he had jealousy in mind. But believe me, jealousy can be a powerful force to advance the kingdom of God—whether in increasing the numbers of His people, preparing sovereign vessels for service, or bringing together events that led His Son to the cross.

As I said above, Paul hoped that the Gentiles' turning to Jesus Christ would make Jews jealous and want salvation through Christ too (Rom. 11:11–14).

The point is, God uses jealousy for His own purposes. The sons of Jesse being jealous of their little brother David was part of David's preparation. It helped get him ready for what was coming down the road. Jealousy is what eventually made Joseph prime minister of Egypt. And the jealousy between Leah and Rachel was no small force in making Jacob the father of twelve sons. God was behind it all. His kingdom was at stake. He used jealousy to ensure that things happened according to His sovereign will.

Leah and Rachel were sisters, but Jacob was married to both of them. It was not Jacob's choice; he was tricked by Laban, who had promised Jacob his daughter Rachel—but at the last minute gave him Leah.

THE UNLOVED WOMAN: LEAH

Leah is possibly one of the most underestimated and unappreciated women in the Bible. She is an example of one whose life was hard but whose eternal reward would more than compensate for her suffering. She is said to have had "weak eyes." This could refer to her eyesight, but possibly mainly to her appearance—that she was very plain, especially when compared to her sister, Rachel. Their father, Laban, took advantage of both Leah and Rachel, and also Jacob, forcing Jacob to take Leah as his wife—fearing (I suppose) that she would not otherwise get married. Laban showed insensitivity to everyone's feelings. A good father would not treat a daughter like that. Leah was manipulated and controlled by an uncaring father.

Laban had promised Jacob that he could have his daughter Rachel as his wife. As part of the agreement, Jacob worked seven years for Laban to get Rachel. The time for the wedding finally arrived. After the wedding banquet, when it was night, Laban put his daughter Leah into a tent, gave her to Jacob, and Jacob lay with her, supposing it was Rachel. "When morning came, there was Leah! So Jacob said to Laban, 'What is this you have done to me? I served you for Rachel, didn't I? Why have you deceived me?'" (Gen. 29:25). It did not cross Jacob's mind also to say, "What have you done to Leah?" Nobody seemed to care about her feelings. Laban's answer: "It is not our custom here to give the younger daughter in marriage before the older one. Finish this daughter's bridal week; then we will give you the younger one also, in return for another seven years of work" (vv. 26–27). The truth is, Jacob never loved or appreciated Leah. She hoped, however, to win his affections, always saying, "Surely my husband will love me now," thinking that giving him children would make the difference. It didn't. She kept having babies, always thinking, "Now at last my husband will become attached to me" (v. 34). He never did.

THE WOMAN WHO HAD EVERYTHING: RACHEL

By today's standards Rachel would be the envy of nearly every woman. "Lovely in form, and beautiful" (Gen. 29:17) suggests she had both a lovely figure and beautiful face. She also was brave and courageous, being a shepherdess—unafraid to be in the wild as she obviously was. She was also clever, as her quick thinking and ability to hide Laban's household gods reveals (Gen. 31:35). Most of all, she had the love, affection, and admiration of her husband. Jacob adored her and regarded working for Laban for seven years "like only a few days to him because of his love for her" (Gen. 29:20). Few women are loved and appreciated like that.

Who would have thought the day would come that Rachel

would be jealous of her plain, unloved, older sister? If you had predicted Rachel would ever be jealous of Leah, no one would have believed you. But she became very jealous indeed of Leah.

In this world not everything is as it seems. You look at people and imagine how happy they must be. "There must be the perfect marriage," you say about a particular couple when, chances are, the truth is that their marriage is a living hell. You look at people with their nice homes and fine cars and imagine how happy they must be. "If only I were in their situation," you say, when chances are, they are totally miserable. You admire a person's gift, opportunities, position, success, intellect, personality, friends, and connections and feel utter envy. The truth so often is, if you knew, you would far, far prefer to have your present situation as opposed to theirs a thousand times over.

I used to work as a door-to-door vacuum cleaner salesman. I worked in the upper class neighborhoods in and around Miami and Fort Lauderdale, Florida, where people could buy my product without applying for credit. I got to know quite a number of these people. Many would confide in me—some of them being very famous in the social and financial world. When I would hear of their problems—the sadness, the brokenness, and the heartaches—I realized how unhappy so many of these people were. "Not all that glitters is gold." And so I realized how much better off I was, although I was very unhappy and embarrassed to be selling vacuum cleaners to make a living. I learned not to be the slightest bit jealous of wealthy people.

And so, as it turns out, Rachel didn't have everything after all. Her beauty and even having a husband's love wasn't enough in her case. It goes to show that appearing to have everything is so often only an illusion. What mattered most to Rachel in the end was wanting the very thing she did not have: the privilege of being a mother. Therefore when Rachel saw that she was not bearing Jacob any children, "she became jealous of her sister. So she said to Jacob, 'Give me children, or I'll die!'" (Gen. 30:1). Her beauty, body, bravery, and brains now meant little to her by comparison. She wanted to have babies.

Mutual Jealousy

A rivalry developed. It was the plain and unloved Leah who had what Rachel didn't have—children. But Leah was jealous of Rachel, who had what Leah didn't have—her husband's love and affection. So Rachel and Leah were jealous of each other. We are all like that. We seem so often to want what the other person has that we think will make us happy and fulfilled—their gift, brains, security, and sense of confidence.

However, Leah's being unloved and unattractive was compensated by her having children. And yet that did not fully satisfy her. The thing that mattered most to Leah was how Jacob felt toward her. The whole time she was bearing children she thought of Jacob and how to win him over. It became an obsession with her. When her firstborn, Reuben, came along she said, "It is because the LORD has seen my misery. Surely my husband will love me now" (Gen. 29:32). When she conceived again, giving birth to Simeon, she said, "Because the LORD heard that I am not loved, he gave me this one too" (v. 33). And when Levi was born, Leah said, "Now at last my husband will become attached to me" (v. 34). She remained unhappy.

Rachel's being barren might have been compensated by Jacob's love for her. But his love was not enough to give her the happiness she craved. The very thing Rachel wanted, Leah had—children. But Leah wanted her husband's affection. The very thing Leah wanted, then, Rachel had—her husband's love. Both women were compensated, but both were unhappy.

It all goes to show that nobody really has everything after all. This life is not perfect—for anybody. We must wait until we get to heaven for that. But in this world there will never be complete happiness. Whether it comes to being loved and appreciated, being attractive or being gifted, we all seem to want something the other person has that we don't have. We seem to want another's success. We want their anointing. We want their personality. We want their intelligence. We want their talent. We want their financial power.

"In this world you will have trouble," said Jesus (John 16:33). "I consider that our present sufferings are not worth comparing with the glory that will be revealed in us," said Paul (Rom. 8:18). "It has been granted to you on behalf of Christ not only to believe on him, but also to suffer for him" (Phil. 1:29). Paul encouraged us not to be unsettled by trials: "You know quite well we were destined for them" (1 Thess. 3:3). God allows just

enough adversity here below that will drive us to seek Him—
and wait for heaven.

The next time you feel jealous and unhappy, remember
that God never intended this present world—with its sin and
misery—to provide perfect happiness for you.

And yet God may allow the jealousy you feel in order to get
your attention—to accomplish what He has in mind for you.
Remember what Martin Luther taught us: God uses sex to drive
one to marriage, ambition to drive one to service, and fear to
drive one to faith. I am sure that God often uses ambition to
motivate us to achieve what God has in mind for us.

Rachel eventually got what she so desperately wanted.
There was an ancient belief that mandrakes would help one's
infertility. Rachel said to Leah, "Give me some of your son's
mandrakes." This annoyed Leah. "Wasn't it enough that you
took away my husband?" This revealed how jealous Leah had
been since, following the night of her marriage to Jacob, she
now accused Rachel of stealing her husband from her! Surely,
it would seem, that Leah must have known the original plan.
But not according to this. She was nursing a grudge against
Rachel all this time. Then she added, "Will you take my son's
mandrakes too?" (Gen. 30:14–15).

It turns out that Rachel kept Jacob largely to herself in
those days. She then made a deal with Leah. "He [Jacob] can
sleep with you tonight in return for your son's mandrakes,"
Rachel pompously and patronizingly said to Leah. Leah then
confronted Jacob—this being not the best way to win him over,

"You must sleep with me...I have hired you with my son's mandrakes." So Jacob slept with Leah (v. 16). More children from Leah followed.

How did the mandrakes work? You tell me. I only know that shortly after this, "God remembered Rachel; he listened to her and opened her womb." She gave birth to a son—Joseph— saying, "God has taken away my disgrace" (vv. 22–23). It also shows that Rachel had been praying to God.

As I said in *Did You Think to Pray?* God likes our company. He comes up with ways to get our attention so that we will spend time with Him. It is reasonable to assume that God wanted Rachel's attention. Her barrenness drove her to her knees. And God answered her. Joseph became Jacob's favorite son and was the sovereign lifeline to the children of Israel in coming years. We may not realize how much our frustrations and hurts—even jealousies—are being used of God for His future kingdom. All I know is, Rachel prayed. She was so desperate. And God heard her.

Rachel had a second son—Benjamin. Sadly, she died when giving birth to him (Gen. 35:16–20). The love of Jacob's life was buried in Bethlehem. The woman who seemed to have everything even gave him two sons—but then died. We simply do not live in a perfect world.

Leah gave Jacob six sons. The unloved woman, however, was compensated by what I can only call an *eternal* reward. Jacob never loved her, and Leah never felt a satisfaction on this earth for what she did in giving him those sons. It is noteworthy that, after hoping each time she gave birth to a son that she would gain Jacob's affection, she finally quit trying. When Judah was born, instead of saying, "Perhaps my husband will love me now," she became resigned. She simply said, "*This time I will praise the* LORD" (Gen. 29:35, emphasis added). Wow.

I find this so moving. She turned her attention away from Jacob. She realized that trying to win him over was hopeless. So she finally gave up...and looked heavenward: "This time I will praise the LORD." As we will see in more detail below, this happens to be one of the best ways to overcome jealousy. Are you desperately jealous? Try praising the Lord.

There are two things here that Leah probably did not realize. First, when she praised the Lord, she truly pleased the Lord. God wanted her affections directed to Him all along. He wanted her to desire His love and approval above Jacob's. I would not be surprised to learn when we get to heaven, that God used Rachel's barrenness to get her attention, and He used Leah's being unloved to get her attention too.

Second, Leah could not have known what she actually did for the kingdom of God and the future of Israel in giving birth to those sons. One of them was Levi. His name would live in honor in Israel forever. The tribe of Levi became the most prestigious in Israel, for out of Levi came the priesthood. The Book of Leviticus was named for him.

But that is not all. Leah gave birth to Judah. From Judah came Israel's greatest king—David, son of Jesse—and most of all, from Judah came God's promised Messiah—our Lord Jesus

Christ, born of the seed of David. That is why I say that Leah was compensated with an eternal reward—one she did not get to enjoy here below but will know in heaven what she did for the kingdom of God.

Sadly, Jacob never appreciated Leah; she possibly did more for Israel at the end of the day than his beloved Rachel ever did. But you could not have told Jacob that.

Do you know what it is to be unloved? Are you an unloved woman? Do you know what it is to be unappreciated?

Bear in mind three things:

1. God likes your company and is doing what He can to get your attention.

2. Your reward and happiness may not come in this life but later on.

3. When you give up on what you so longed for, you might follow Leah's example—and just praise the Lord.

The best cure for jealousy is to praise the Lord.

Chapter Five

EVIL JEALOUSY

"Here comes that dreamer!" they said to each other. "Come now, let's kill him.... Then we'll see what comes of his dreams."

—Genesis 37:19–20

Because the patriarchs were jealous of Joseph, they sold him as a slave into Egypt. But God was with him and rescued him from all his troubles.

—Acts 7:9–10

You meant evil against me, but God meant it for good.

—Genesis 50:20, esv

IT REALLY IS amazing how often God uses jealousy to advance His purposes. God turns evil into good, overruling the worst in people and the lowest of motives to further His aim in a fallen world. The bottom line of the Book of Job, for example, is this—I am thrilled every time I think of it: "I know that you can do all things; *no plan of yours can be thwarted*," said Job (Job 42:2, emphasis added). That is perhaps the greatest thing Job learned in all his suffering: no plan of God can ultimately be thwarted. I wonder, however, how many of us really do believe that? I can only say that I have found it true again and again. I can think of the many, many times I have messed up, stuck my foot in it, let God down, made the angels blush, offended a friend unnecessarily, made an unguarded comment, completely lost my head, or made a bad choice—only to see God overrule. Note: I said overrule. He steps in, rolls up His sleeves, negates—as if He overlooks—what I did. Despite how foolish and stupid I was, He lets me save face. God often has to do this. It is as though He works overtime to undo the bad stuff I have done.

Whereas there was nothing good about his brothers' jealousy, it is nonetheless true that had not Joseph's brothers been jealous of him, he would never have become the prime minister of Egypt or the instrument of preserving the family of Israel in a time of great famine. That does not mean that Joseph was justified for his foolish arrogance; it shows how God can overrule one's folly. There was nothing right about his brothers' jealousy, but God used it for His glory.

Joseph had become Jacob's favorite son. He was treated like the firstborn. Jacob made a "richly ornamented robe" for Joseph (Gen. 37:3—"coat of many colours," KJV). The only thing worse than Jacob making the robe was Joseph wearing it—which he did—in front of his brothers. Utterly insensitive to their feelings, Joseph arrogantly strutted around in that robe as if he were a crown prince and a cut above them all. He thought he was better than they. Not only that; he was an obnoxious, poisonous tattletale and did absolutely nothing to endear himself to his brothers.

But there is more. Unfair as it may seem, God Himself endowed Joseph with an unusual gift; it had to do with dreams and interpretation of dreams. The gifts and calling of God are without repentance—irrevocable (Rom. 11:29). This means they are sovereignly bestowed, certainly not because of our good works but because God has mercy on whom He will (Exod. 33:19). In a word: we do nothing to earn such a gift; moreover, that gift may remain intact regardless of one's obedience to God. (This explains why one's gift may flourish parallel with one's moral failure.) Why God would bestow a remarkable spiritual gift to such a conceited young man is beyond most people's sense of justice, and yet God does that sort of thing.

God gave Joseph prophetic dreams. Furthermore, the dreams indicated that these brothers would one day bow down to him. That is not all; Joseph *told* the dreams—to his brothers! What a foolish thing to do. He didn't have to do that! "Listen to this dream I had: We were binding sheaves of grain out in the field when suddenly my sheaf rose and stood upright, while your sheaves gathered around mine and bowed down to it." No need for a Sigmund Freud to interpret this dream! They replied, "'Do you intend to reign over us? Will you actually rule us?' And they hated him all the more because of his dream and what he had said" (Gen. 37:5–8).

Joseph did not know when to stop. "I had another dream, and this time the sun and moon and eleven stars were bowing down to me" (v. 9). You didn't need to be an expert dream interpreter to interpret that one either. This one even gave Jacob pause. "What is this dream you had? Will your mother and I and your brothers actually come and bow down to the ground before you?" (v. 10).

Joseph's mistake was telling his dreams. He was certainly not required to tell everything God showed him! But he did. I sometimes think God would reveal more than He does to many of us if we were not so intent on telling everybody. The psalmist says that God "confides" in those who fear Him (Ps. 25:14), which suggests He doesn't want us to blab to the world everything He shows us. Perhaps He would tell us more if we could keep quiet about it.

> His brothers were jealous of him, but his father kept
> the matter in mind.
>
> —Genesis 37:11

There was nothing wrong with Joseph's gift, but there was a lot wrong with Joseph. He would need sorting out. He was destined to be a future prime minister of Egypt, but he was far from ready for that.

Productive Jealousy

Perhaps you have an unusual gift. Let us say that there is nothing wrong with your gift, but could it be there is something wrong with *you*? Could it be that you are not ready for the task to which God has called you? You like Joseph would therefore need disciplining, sometimes called chastening. After all, for whom the Lord loves He disciplines (Heb. 12:6). This comes from a Greek word that means "enforced learning." Chastening is essentially painful preparation. It is not, however, a case of "tit for tat"—of God getting even with us for our past mistakes. God got even at the cross! "As far as the east is from the west, so far has he removed our transgressions from us" (Ps. 103:12). The blood of Jesus Christ washes away our sins (expiation) and turns God's wrath away from our sins (propitiation). Chastening, therefore, is not tit for tat but rather preparation for future usefulness. If chastening were tit for tat, we would be chastened all the time! Thank God it is not tit for tat. He disciplines us because He is not finished with us yet, that we might be partakers of His holiness—in order to produce in us a harvest of righteousness (Heb. 12:10–11).

One of the chief ways God refines, or chastens, us is by forcing us to cope with jealousy—sometimes our own and sometimes somebody else's. When it is our own, it can be what I earlier called productive jealousy, as in Ecclesiastes 4:4—when we are motivated to want to improve our situation because of envy. But one of the main ways God also uses jealousy is when He allows us to have to cope with another's jealousy. The purpose is to let us suffer the pain of their venom—as it was in the case of Joseph. It is when someone is determined to hurt us—our reputation or livelihood. What good does it do? For one thing, it keeps us on our knees! It forces us to cry out to God. God can use another's jealousy to get our attention—to make us pray when we had not been praying, to seek His face when we had not been reading His Word, and to trust Him alone when we had been relying on ourselves. Another person's jealousy is one of God's favorite weapons to make us more like Jesus.

When I first started out in the ministry back in 1954, an old evangelist from Kentucky—who also went by his initials—C. B. Fuggitt said to me: "RT, every compliment, every bouquet, every accolade I ever got did little or nothing to increase my anointing; but every kick, every jolt, every lie about me, and every jealous word resulted in my being blessed beyond measure."

I have discovered that this has been largely true with me too. I appreciate compliments (perhaps too much), and I do know that (at times) God used a timely word of encouragement when I needed it. But I would have to say that, as I am now in my seventies, speaking personally, even though I believe in taking advantage of every opportunity to increase one's anointing— whether by dignifying trials, total forgiveness, increasing your prayer life, or getting prayed for through the laying on of hands—any success that has come my way can be traced almost entirely to my being hurt by another's jealousy and the way I coped with it. That is simply my opinion, even if I am speculating a bit.

Joseph's brothers were all set to take his life. "Let's kill him and throw him into one of these cisterns and say that a ferocious animal devoured him. Then we'll see what comes of his dreams" (Gen. 37:20). They decided to throw him into a cistern, but not before they stripped him of that coat of many colors. This was part of Joseph's preparation. The first thing to go was the "sore spot"—that robe.

Perhaps many of us have a sore spot that needs to be dealt with as part of our preparation. It may be the rough edges of our personality, the refusal to get help, the unwillingness to get more education or training, the rejection of advice, the inability to handle money, holding a grudge, or a grumbling spirit. In the case of Joseph, he needed to forgive his brothers for what they ended up doing. They were going to leave him in a pit to die in, but providentially some Ishmaelites turned up at the same moment and bought Joseph as a slave for twenty shekels of silver. The brothers took Joseph's robe, dipped it in blood, and lay it before old Jacob, who took the bait: "Joseph has surely been torn to pieces...in mourning will I go down to the grave to my son" (Gen. 37:33–35).

I have compared my own preparation with that of Joseph in this way: my grandmother had bought me a brand-new car in 1955 when, as a student at Trevecca Nazarene University, I became the pastor of a Nazarene church in Palmer, Tennessee, 115 miles from Nashville. I look back on how insensitive I must have been and (almost certainly) how I made so many students jealous by having that car. Very few students had cars in those days. That car was a "sore spot." But in 1956 my grandmother, seeing as she did that I was not going to please her in all my future plans, took the car back! The "sore spot" was the first to go. This happened at the beginning of a long era—lasting several years—of God disciplining me and preparing me. But down the road there would be countless sore spots God would have to deal with before I could be entrusted with a ministry.

When people are a little bit jealous of you, there is probably not a lot you can do about it. If their envy is mild, sometimes you can warm up to them and win them over. But when people are extremely jealous of you, as Joseph's brothers were, there is nothing you can do about it. You cannot make people like you. I have known one or two cases when I suspected that someone's stated objections to my theology almost certainly masked their real problem—jealousy. I knew, therefore, that even if I changed my theology they would feel the same way toward me. When you know in your heart of hearts the real problem is their jealousy of you, you are helpless. There is not a thing on earth you can do.

Except forgive.

Total Forgiveness Overcomes Jealousy

Over forty years ago there were two churches with similar names in Fort Lauderdale, Florida: Coral Ridge Baptist Church, which started first, and Coral Ridge Presbyterian Church, which appeared almost overnight. The Baptist church had about twenty-five people attending; the latter, led by Dr. D. James Kennedy, experienced phenomenal growth—several thousand. The pastor of the Baptist church at the time, sadly, lamented the growth of the Presbyterian church—and came up with what to him was a shocking revelation—and proof that people should not attend Dr. Kennedy's church: that Dr. Kennedy was actually an amillennialist! (That is the view that the one thousand years in Revelation 20 is not to be taken literally.) He spread this word around as if to warn people from attending a heretical church. Everybody could see, however, that there was an underlying problem in the Baptist pastor, one that had nothing to do with eschatology! But jealousy can make us say silly things.

When your enemy is motivated by jealousy, you will not change them, you cannot make them like you, you probably cannot convince them their problem is jealousy (you look foolish if you do), and you cannot nudge the arm of providence or get other people to make them see their folly. "A man convinced against his will is of the same opinion still." There is only one thing you can do. Forgive them.

It is not what they think of you that matters; it is what you think of them. Envy rots the bones (Prov. 14:30); don't let it rot your bones. Forgive them. Totally.

Joseph certainly tried to judge the arm of providence. It was when he was falsely accused of trying to rape the wife of Potiphar—the Egyptian officer for whom he worked—and put in prison (Gen. 39). When Joseph unexpectedly had an opportunity to exercise his gift of interpreting dreams, he exploited it. He prophesied to Pharaoh's chief cupbearer, in prison with Joseph, that this cupbearer would be restored to his job in three days. So far, so good. But Joseph could not resist adding a personal, manipulative word to the cupbearer. "When all goes well with you, remember me and show me kindness; mention me to Pharaoh and get me out of this prison. For I was forcibly carried off from the land of the Hebrews, and even here I have done nothing to deserve being put in a dungeon" (Gen. 40:14–15).

I reckon that God looked down from heaven and said, "Oh, Joseph, I wish you hadn't said that. You are going to need a couple of more years in prison." Part of Joseph's preparation was to forgive not only his brothers, Potiphar's wife (for the false accusation), Potiphar (for believing his wife's lie), Jacob (for being an unwise parent), and even God (for letting all this happen)—but also the cupbearer, who "did not remember Joseph; he forgot him" (Gen. 40:23). Joseph's preparation consisted not only of totally forgiving everybody who had hurt him but also to wait for God's time to come! Joseph needed to see that God would bring about all He promised without Joseph lifting a little finger!

When we are victims of another's jealousy, all we can do is to forgive that person for his or her jealousy. Such forgiveness must be from the heart. You must truly mean it.

Total forgiveness means that they are off the hook; they aren't going to get caught or exposed. We pray that God will even bless them *as though they did nothing to us.*

Joseph knew that his dreams would be eventually fulfilled. He knew that one day these brothers would come begging to him. They would bow. But Joseph probably also assumed this meant he would be able to look at them and say, "Gotcha!"

Perhaps you too are the victim of jealousy. You have been

crushed. Your spirit is broken. People believe the lie that has been perpetrated. Your reputation has been injured. Your future is bleak. You cry out to God for vindication. Perhaps you have had a dream that you will be vindicated. Perhaps you were given a prophetic word. Could it be that God has promised that He would use you one day? You have waited and waited. You cry out, "How long? How long? How long? How long?"

Could I suggest to you just how long it will be? I venture to say: as long as it takes to bring you to the very same place Joseph finally came to. He totally forgave everybody who let him down, especially those who had been jealous of him.

How do we know this? Because on the day when the dreams were finally fulfilled, instead of Joseph saying "Gotcha!" and throwing the book at them (which he used to imagine he would do—and which he could have done), he totally forgave them.

Here is what happened. Joseph's time finally came. The cupbearer remembered Joseph when none other than Pharaoh himself had dreams nobody could interpret. Joseph was brought in before Pharaoh. He not only interpreted Pharaoh's dreams, but he also told the king exactly what to do—which would ensure that Egypt would become very wealthy in a time of famine (Gen. 41:28–40). The Pharaoh made Joseph prime minister of Egypt overnight. When the famine took place, Joseph's brothers came from Canaan to purchase food. They had to face the prime minister, not knowing it was Joseph himself. The dreams were fulfilled. His brothers bowed down to him. But instead of throwing the book at them, he blessed them.

The only sure and never-to-be-regretted way to cope with another's jealousy is by demonstrating total forgiveness. And yet total forgiveness is a spiritual state to which all of us are already called (Matt. 5:44; Luke 6:27–28; Eph. 4:32). If it takes their jealousy to bring you to attain to this, thank God for it. If you are like me, demonstrating total forgiveness was long overdue in any case. So if it takes another's jealousy for God to get your attention, thank Him! Seize the opportunity with both hands.

If you ask, "How do I know I have totally forgiven those who have hurt me?" I reply, follow Joseph's example.

1. You don't tell anybody what they did to you. When Joseph made himself known to his brothers, he ordered everybody present to leave the room so that nobody in Egypt would ever find out what his brothers had done (Gen. 45:1–2).

2. You won't let them be fearful of you. "Come close to me," Joseph said to his brothers; he was determined to put them at ease (Gen. 45:3–4).

3. You don't want them to feel guilty. "Do not be distressed and do not be angry with yourselves" (Gen. 45:5).

4. You let them save face. This means protecting their fragile egos; you cover for them, making them feel

good, not bad. "It was not you who sent me here, but God" (Gen. 45:8).

5. You protect them from their darkest secret. Joseph's brothers would prefer death to having to tell their father the truth of what they did, so Joseph did not allow them to tell him (Gen. 45:9–13).

6. You don't do it merely once; you do it for the rest of your life. Seventeen years later their father died, and the brothers concocted a story because they feared Joseph would get vengeance on them once Jacob died. They were wrong; Joseph really *had* forgiven them and kept it up (Gen. 50:15–21).

Total forgiveness is a life sentence; you do it as long as you live. I have elaborated on these six points (and many more principles) in *Total Forgiveness*.

The real genius of Joseph was not his gifting but in the fact that he really *had* forgiven them! It was genuine forgiveness, not a quick, glossing over, makeshift position to get God's favor; he had really, completely, truly, and totally forgiven them. This is why Joseph could be trusted with greatness. It is why greatness is graciously withheld from us by our loving Father; we would certainly misuse and abuse the position if we should get exalted before we are truly ready. As Dr. Martyn Lloyd-Jones used to say to me: the worst thing that can happen to a man is to succeed before he is ready. Joseph was ready. He did not let their jealousy destroy him at the end of the day.

That is the challenge you and I face: don't let their jealousy make your bones rot. As Nelson Mandela once put it: when you are bitter, you give them your heart and soul; don't give them those two things. Just forgive them instead. Totally.

Chapter Six

PETTY JEALOUSY

When Eliab, David's oldest brother, heard him speaking with the men, he burned with anger at him and asked, "Why have you come down here? And with whom did you leave those few sheep in the desert? I know how conceited you are and how wicked your heart is; you came down only to watch the battle.

—1 SAMUEL 17:28

Resentment kills a fool, and envy slays the simple.

—JOB 5:2

IN EARLY 1964, after my ministry was rejected by a small church in Ohio, Louise and I returned to Florida for me to sell vacuum cleaners again. I found a new friend—Bill— who also had been rejected by his church in New Jersey. We met at a Presbyterian church in Fort Lauderdale. He needed a job. I taught him how to sell vacuum cleaners door-to-door. Those were difficult days for both of us, feeling the embarrassment of being out of the ministry and working as salesmen, but we became close friends. We were much the same age, but he had a seminary education—not me (at that time). I felt inferior to him. He had a benign way of letting me know I was uneducated compared to him. I felt jealous.

The nearest I ever came to experiencing sibling rivalry was with Bill. It was Bill who started me fishing in the Florida Keys. He was a superb fisherman. When I began learning how to bonefish, he would always laugh at my inability to catch my first one. I refused to hire a fishing guide, and I went fishing virtually every week for nearly ten months without success. The phone would ring on Saturday evenings about the time I would return from fishing. Bill would say, "I bet you didn't catch any—again." It galvanized me like no force I had known in years! When I finally caught one, he was the first I wanted to tell. And I kept telling him as I got better at it. It was so good for me. There is no doubt: I would *never* have been so gripped by bonefishing apart from Bill's chiding me, strange as this may seem. He caught several bonefish long before I did. It made me *so* jealous! But I have always seen it as providential. Bonefishing, which I became fairly good at, subsequently made for me more friendships, created more strategic situations for future ministry, and has given me more pleasure than you could possibly imagine.

Whether David's brother Eliab's hurtful comment—"I know how conceited you are and how wicked your heart is"—galvanized David, who knows? But shortly afterward young David went to King Saul to offer his services to fight the giant

Goliath—and he killed him. I would not be surprised if David thought to himself, holding Goliath's head high before all Israel, "I wonder what Eliab thinks now."

Israel had been running scared in the face of Goliath's challenge, "I defy the ranks of Israel! Give me a man and let us fight each other." The Israelites were "dismayed and terrified" (1 Sam. 17:10–11). But not David. Having learned what the reward would be for killing Goliath—marrying the king's daughter and the family being exempt from taxes—David went to the king. "Let no one lose heart on account of this Philistine; your servant will go and fight him" (v. 32).

Eliab had been passed over by Samuel to be the next king. When Samuel went to the house of Jesse to anoint the next king, he hastily assumed it would be Eliab, Jesse's firstborn son. "Surely the LORD's anointed stands here before the LORD," believing it was Eliab. But God intervened and said to Samuel, "Do not consider his appearance or his height, for I have rejected him. The LORD does not look at the things man looks at. Man looks at the outward appearance, but the LORD looks at the heart" (1 Sam. 16:6–7).

Jesse then called each of his sons—all of seven of them—except young David. This is quite amazing. Jesse did not even inform David that the great prophet Samuel was on the premises. David was completely ignored by his father. You can be fairly sure that there was no jealousy toward David at this stage. David was then regarded as insignificant and irrelevant. When Samuel was not convinced he had met the right person, he turned to Jesse, "Are these all the sons you have?" (v. 11). Samuel must have thought that his prophetic gift had failed him. "There is still the youngest," Jesse replied to Samuel—as if to talk him out of pursuing David, "but he is tending the sheep" (v. 11).

It is not likely, therefore, that the seven sons of Jesse were jealous of young David up to then—who was a shepherd. The youngest brother who looked after sheep was probably no threat to the self-esteem of Eliab and the other brothers.

People are normally not jealous of those who are inferior to them. Not only that, but when you have everything, you are not easily threatened. While I was writing this book, Tim Russert, the beloved host of the television program *Meet the Press*, died. It was big news. For five days the networks kept talking about Tim Russert. The comment came, "He knew no envy." That is, everybody said he wasn't jealous of anybody. I'm quite sure I believe it. But Tim Russert was at the very top of his profession and the most popular telecaster in America. People like this don't tend to get jealous! It is not that they are free of jealousy; they simply stay unchallenged.

But when Samuel insisted that they bring David in from tending the sheep—and then David got anointed by the great Samuel—David suddenly became a target of jealousy. Things would never be the same again.

WHEN THEY ARE ENVIOUS OF YOUR ANOINTING

There is nothing that will make people more jealous of you than your anointing. Your anointing will make you a threat.

It is good to be reminded that the anointing is a word that refers to the power of the Spirit to make you do what you are good at—with amazing ease. Like killing Goliath. Or prophesying. Or preaching. Teaching. Understanding computers. Making money. Leading people.

People will not be jealous of you when you lose your job, lose income, fail in school, don't get the promotion, get turned down, don't get invited, aren't very popular, aren't regarded as very talented or intelligent, don't get recognized, and don't live in an attractive location or drive a nice car. When people like this have a bit of bad luck, others will say, "Poor John; I feel *so* sorry for him." They will even get a pious feeling that they show such compassion. But it has nothing to do with compassion; it has largely to do with the absence of a threat.

David was no threat in the sheep pens from which God chose him (Ps. 78:70). Jesse's seven sons would not struggle with jealousy toward David as long as it was young David the shepherd. But the anointing oil on David from Samuel changed everything. "So Samuel took the horn of oil and anointed him in the presence of his brothers, and from that day on the Spirit of the LORD came upon David in power" (1 Sam. 16:13). David would never be viewed the same way by his brothers again.

We will even feel sorry for the person who has everything—if he loses it! We may inwardly gloat. But outwardly we say, "I am *so* sorry to hear that you lost all that money." We lie.

When Billy Graham preached for us at Westminster Chapel, he had to go to the hospital in London on the Saturday before. It was in all the newspapers. The word spread that Billy would have to cancel preaching at Westminster Chapel. On the Sunday morning I received a phone call from someone who had been most unhappy that Dr. Graham was scheduled to preach for us. They phoned to say, "We are *so* sorry, RT, so *very* sorry indeed—that Billy Graham won't be with you today." I replied, "Oh, yes, he will. I just talked with him. He will stay in the hospital all day, then come to the chapel tonight just in time to preach—then return to the hospital." Silence. "Oh," they replied. Their thinly veiled disappointment that Billy was still coming to us was embarrassing. "I am very happy for you," they unconvincingly said. And hung up.

It takes minimal grace to weep with those who weep; it takes a lot of grace to rejoice with those who rejoice. "Do not gloat when your enemy falls; when he stumbles, do not let your heart rejoice, or the LORD will see and disapprove and turn his wrath away from him" (Prov. 24:17–18). The most natural reaction in the world is to gloat when your enemy has something bad happen to him. But Proverbs 24:18 is a solemn warning not to do this. You should fight against gloating when your enemy falls just as you do resisting any other kind of temptation from the flesh. Jealousy has a way of creeping in when we aren't aware what is happening. The heart is so deceitful (Jer. 17:9).

I have wondered how David felt about his own father not even going to tell him that the great Samuel had come to their home. He may have wondered why his brothers did not step in and say, "Aren't you going to send for David too?"

The wonderful thing was, God knew where David was. Jesse knew too, of course, but he had no plans to bring David into the equation. God overruled. It was to Samuel's everlasting credit that he stuck to his guns and did not settle on one of Jesse's sons since he had expressly come there to anoint one of them. You may feel like David at times. Perhaps your parents underestimated you or preferred a different brother or sister. Perhaps you were not included in a great opportunity that was extended to others. David would have missed the big service! Have you had people say to you, "You missed a great service Sunday," and you feel pretty awful that God would show up powerfully in church when you weren't there? You wondered if God cares about you—to let you be absent when the power of God was present. David could have felt like that.

But God found David. "I have found David son of Jesse a man after my own heart; he will do everything I want him to do" (Acts 13:22).

He will find you too.

LET JEALOUSY BE A GOOD SIGN TO YOU

Eliab wanted to cut David down to size. Several hurtful things flowed from Eliab's bitter jealousy of David. First, Eliab began by saying, "Why have you come down here?... You came down

101

only to watch the battle" (1 Sam. 17:28). That was wrong, which of course David knew. Eliab thus questioned David's motives in showing up in the middle of the Israelites' battle with Goliath. It is painful when those close to you question your motives. The truth is, David was only being obedient to his father (v. 18). But when the accusations are out-and-out lies, you may know that the origin of the attack is the devil.

Never take persecution personally. It is not you they hate; it is Christ in you. It is God they hate.

There is a striking comparison between David and Jesus here. David, like Joseph, was often what is called a "type of Christ"—one who makes you think of Jesus long before Jesus was ever born.

For example, Jesus's motives were questioned by His brothers too. They accused Him of vain ambition, as if He was wanting to become famous and had a need to make a name for Himself. "You ought to leave here and go to Judea, so that your disciples may see the miracles you do. No one who wants to become a public figure acts in secret," they said to him (John 7:3–4). What a put-down! Since Jesus was tempted at all points, as we are (Heb. 4:15, KJV), it is encouraging to know how He can sympathize indeed with us when our motives are questioned by people, especially when their real problem is jealousy. Jesus always and only did what was in obedience to His Father. "The Son can do nothing by himself; he can do only what he sees his Father doing" (John 5:19). If we do only what the Father instructs us to do, you can be sure people will be jealous of us—and question our motives. But we can cope when we know in our hearts we have done what the Father told us to do.

The second thing Eliab said to David was, "With whom did you leave those few sheep in the desert?" (1 Sam. 17:28). It was another put-down, minimizing his responsibility and significance. He was a shepherd, yes. But he only had a "few sheep." When people are jealous of you, they will undermine any success or dignity you have.

Jesus's enemies seized not on the number but the quality of His disciples. Jesus welcomed tax collectors and sinners (Matt. 9:11; Luke 15:1–2). What was meant to make Jesus look bad really gave Jesus an opportunity to explain His mission. "It is not the healthy who need a doctor, but the sick. . . . I have not come to call the righteous, but sinners" (Matt. 9:12–13). Jesus was never ashamed of His following.

David would later face this sort of attack—in a different way. His wife Michal was incensed that David welcomed slave girls to dance with him when bringing the ark into Jerusalem. It was an attack on David's dignity. He replied to her, "I will become even more undignified than this, and I will be humiliated in my own eyes. But by these slave girls you spoke of, I will be held in honor" (2 Sam. 6:22).

Thirdly, Eliab claimed to know the status of David's heart and character—"I know how conceited you are and how wicked your heart is" (1 Sam. 17:28). What a horrible thing to say to the seventeen-year-old David who had just been anointed by the prophet Samuel. But when your enemies resort to personal attacks like that, mark it down: they have run out of ammunition. They are desperate to hurt you. The battle won't be long now. Victory is at hand. In David's case, moments later he was fully vindicated. As for Eliab, we never hear of him again.

Those who are jealous of you will fade into insignificance. It is only a matter of time. You will be able to say with David—who was probably referring to King Saul, whom we will examine next: "I have seen a wicked and ruthless man flourishing like a green tree in its native soil, but he soon passed away and was no more; though I looked for him, he could not be found" (Ps. 37:35–36).

When people are jealous of you, take it as a sign—a good sign—that God is preparing you for something important down the road. Yes, take that sign with both hands. It hurts for a while, but it will bring to birth a new person in you. As Jesus put it, "You will grieve, but your grief will turn to joy. A woman giving birth to a child has pain because her time has come; but when her baby is born she forgets the anguish because of her joy that a child is born into the world" (John 16:20–21).

The birth of the child that is coming is worth waiting for.

Chapter Seven

RIDICULING JEALOUSY

For even his own brothers did not believe in him.
—JOHN 7:5

It is not love that is blind, but jealousy.[1]
—LAWRENCE DURRELL

The dogs bark, the caravan marches on.
—ARABIC PROVERB

JESUS UNDERSTANDS SIBLING rivalry better than anybody you will meet.

As I said earlier, when I first decided I must write this book I did not realize how many of the numerous biblical examples of jealousy and envy would actually pertain to sibling rivalry. It has given me pause and has made me see more than ever the pain and frustration so many have felt, which I myself have hardly experienced. My sister, Marilyn, came along when I was fifteen. She could write my biography and call it *My Brother Was an Only Child*.

But there is one who *does* understand what you are going through if your own problem with jealousy has largely to do with a brother or sister. The writer of the epistle to the Hebrews said, "For we do not have a high priest who is unable to sympathize with our weaknesses, but we have one who has been *tempted in every way*, just as we are—yet was without sin" (Heb. 4:15, emphasis added). Or as the King James Version put it, Jesus was "in all points tempted like as we are." He sympathizes if only because He experienced trial and temptation Himself. The Greek word for temptation—*peirazo*—equally means "tested" or "tried."

There are, however, certain areas of Jesus's temptations some can hardly understand. For example, they cannot figure out how Jesus would be tempted, tested, or tried with regard to old age since He never lived to old age. How can He sympathize with a man in his seventies when Jesus died young? But He does! I myself need to feel these days that He is *touched* with the feeling of my anxieties in this area—as I know He is. I never expected to get old. I always thought the Second Coming would have taken place by now. In a similar way, many also can't figure out how Jesus was coming "soon" two thousand years ago. (I just returned from Northern Ireland. There is a wall by the main road in the little town of Moira, where I stayed, that has in bold letters, "THE COMING OF THE LORD DRAWETH NIGH." My driver, in his fifties, said he can remember that sign when he was a child. That sign made me smile. I thought they might at least change "draweth" to "draws," even if the Second Coming is delayed for another hundred years.) But now that I am in my seventies, believe it or not, I still believe that Jesus *is* coming soon, and likewise that He is touched with the feeling of my old age weaknesses, even though He died at the age of thirty-three.

JESUS AND SIBLING RIVALRY

When it comes to sibling rivalry, we have an expressed, explicit, and revealing account in John 7:1–5 that shows how Jesus's brothers were jealous of Him. It indicates how Jesus Himself understands jealousy from firsthand experience. His brothers were very jealous of Him indeed.

This was part of Jesus's preparation. Some of the most difficult verses in the Bible are these: "He had to be made like his brothers [meaning all of us] in every way, in order that he might become a merciful and faithful high priest in service to God, and that he might make atonement for the sins of the people" (Heb. 2:17). "Although he was a son, he learned obedience from what he suffered" (Heb. 5:8). These verses tell us that Jesus became perfect through suffering. Part of His suffering was in those years of preparation as He grew up in Nazareth.

Jesus's brothers of course were His half-brothers, since Joseph, who is said to be Jesus's father, was not His natural father but adopted father. God Himself was Jesus's Father. Jesus was born of the Virgin Mary without an earthly father (Matt. 1:18–25; Luke 1:30–35). It is also plausible, according to some legends, that Joseph was a widower with sons when he was first engaged to Mary. This would mean not only that Jesus's brothers were a few years older than He but also that His brothers were brothers by adoption. It does not matter whether they were the sons of Mary, making them younger half-brothers, or whether they were sons of Joseph, making them older adopted brothers. The point is, they are *called* His brothers, and that is the way they saw themselves. In any case, Jesus's brothers would not have known of His miraculous birth. Only Joseph and Mary knew this. Mary apparently kept many things a carefully guarded secret for a long time (Luke 2:51).

One of those brothers was James. He is called "the Lord's brother" by the apostle Paul (Gal. 1:19). In his epistle James refers to himself only as "a servant of God and of the Lord Jesus Christ" (James 1:1). Jude was also one of Jesus's brothers, although Jude merely calls himself a "servant of Jesus Christ and a brother of James" (Jude 1). Two of Jesus's brothers thus wrote letters in the New Testament, and James himself was at one stage arguably the most respected leader in the earliest church—even more so than Peter. Their being known as Jesus's brothers apparently gave them a very lofty stature indeed, especially James. (See Acts 12:17; 15:13; 21:18; Gal. 2:9, 12). In other words, Jesus's brothers do not exploit their filial relationship to Jesus but only the way they eventually related to Him—at the level of the Spirit. Jesus was their Lord and their God. And as we will see, they obviously had come a long, long way.

This is quite remarkable. James and Jude thus grew up in Nazareth as Jesus's brothers, and they are no doubt implicated in the account given in John 7:1–5. But in their epistles, rather than refer to their stature as being brothers of Jesus, they call themselves His servants. A mighty transformation had occurred. They mostly cherished their spiritual tie rather than their earthly tie. They were *saved* by faith in Him. This shows that you and I can be as close to Jesus spiritually as they were. They needed to be regenerated (born again) just as we do. Once they saw Him as the Lord Jesus Christ, that is what mattered most to them! It is being born of the Spirit that gives us all status and identity in the family of God.

To put it another way, Jesus is our heavenly Father's only "natural" son. Jesus is God's "one and only Son" (John 3:16). And yet you and I are "children of God" (John 1:12), "sons of God" (Rom. 8:14). How is this possible that you and I can be sons and daughters of the one and only true God? The answer is: by adoption. You and I have been adopted into God's family (Eph. 1:4–5). Not only that; we are "co-heirs with Christ" (Rom. 8:17). This means we have the same rights and security as children of God as if we were God's natural children. This is why Jesus is called "the firstborn of many brothers" (v. 29).

This therefore means that Jesus is our brother. He is your brother and my brother. We have the exact same relationship to Him as James and Jude had—that is, at the spiritual level. This is why they no longer exploited their earthly, filial relationship with Him—refusing to capitalize on it—but regarded Jesus as their Lord and Savior.

Yes indeed, they had come a long way.

So let us now look at the account described by John:

Jesus went around in Galilee, purposely staying away
from Judea because the Jews were waiting to take his
life. But when the Jewish Feast of Tabernacles was
near, Jesus' brothers said to him, "You ought to leave
here and go to Judea, so that your disciples may see
the miracles you do. No one who wants to become a
public figure acts in secret. Since you are doing these
things, show yourself to the world." For even his own
brothers did not believe in him.

—JOHN 7:1–5

This probably means that Jesus had left Capernaum for a
while and went to His hometown in Nazareth—where His
brothers still lived—to escape being apprehended by certain
Jews who were wanting to kill Him. But His brothers made
some strange suggestions to Him. They were cutting, hurtful,
and even hateful comments. They themselves later went to Jerusalem for the Feast of the Tabernacles, which shows they were
religious Jews who lived by the Mosaic Law.

Here is what we can further deduce from John's account:

1. His brothers knew that Jesus performed miracles.

2. They accused Him of vain ambition—of wanting
   mainly to become famous and important.

3. They were not His disciples.

It is not clear whether they knew the Jews were trying to kill Him. For if they did, their coaxing Him to go to the feast would mean they hoped He would get killed. This is not likely; they merely wanted to bring Him down to size, say what was most patronizing and unhelpful—because they were so very, very jealous of Him.

Two Kinds of Faith

The fact that His brothers knew Jesus performed miracles but could speak so disrespectfully to Him shows how a person can believe in the existence of the supernatural and not be saved. There are millions of people who have believed in the miracles of Jesus, including many Muslims, but in order to be *saved* one must believe He is the Son of God. In other words, believing in Jesus's miracles is not enough to indicate saving faith. His brothers apparently took it for granted that Jesus performed miracles. So did the five thousand who feasted on the loaves and fish Jesus provided, but they deserted Him after that (John 6:66).

My reference to saving faith will bear further explaining. Speaking generally, there are two kinds of faith: temporal faith and saving faith. Temporal faith is asking God to take care of your temporal needs. A lot of people do that, even those who say they don't believe in God. General Douglas MacArthur used to say, "There are no atheists in foxholes." In other words, asking God to help you when you are in difficulty does not mean you are saved. God may even answer your prayer, but that does not mean you are saved. Only saving faith saves. That is when you transfer the trust you have had in your good works and best efforts and put that trust in Jesus Christ—God's one and only Son who died on the cross for your sins. That is saving faith: trusting Jesus's blood, not your best efforts. It is the kind of faith that Jesus's own brothers would eventually come to if they hoped to get to heaven one day. As we know, they did come to this later on. But at the time they were accusing Jesus of worldly aspirations, they were a long way from being saved.

Their detached and aloof manner of referring to His disciples—"your disciples"—as people who might enjoy seeing His miracles showed that they had absolutely no part in His ministry. They must have known that Jesus had a following. The word *disciple* does not necessarily refer to the Twelve but only means "follower." Judea was the more prestigious part of ancient Israel, so His brothers were feigning an interest in how He might become better known.

The heart of their cutting comments was that they accused Him of wanting to "make it big" in Israel. They imputed Him with a worldly, carnal, and vain ambition—as if Jesus wanted significance. They were reckoning Jesus with the lowest and basest of motives—that He only wanted to become an important person, a political figure, a public personality. "No one who wants to become a public figure"—implying this is what Jesus wants—"acts in secret," that is, performing miracles in Nazareth where nobody would be taken very seriously. It is like saying to a budding musician who lives in a remote place, "You need to give a concert in the Royal Albert Hall in London or

Carnegie Hall in New York City if you want to become world famous." Their implying that this is what motivated Jesus was their way of saying to Him, "We don't believe in You—we see right through You."

When one has followed the Gospel of John up to this point (John 7:1–5) and gotten to know what really lay behind Jesus's motives, one sees the polar opposite description of what drove Jesus when His brothers spoke as they did. Here is one who was utterly devoted to His Father's will and glory. Here was God's only Son who was consumed with the honor and praise of God alone and not from men. Here is one whose only aim was to finish the work God gave Him to do, namely, to die on the cross and pay our debt to God for us. But what do Jesus's brothers say Jesus is all about? They said He lived for one thing: to become well known in Israel—a public figure.

Their jealousy blinded them to what Jesus was all about. They could not cope with the stir He was making in Galilee. And yet it no doubt went back many years as they watched Him grow up in Nazareth. We must avoid speculation as to whether Jesus grew up performing miracles. We have no idea what His relationship to His parents was like, except that He was an obedient son (Luke 2:51). There can be no doubt that He was different from them—perhaps in the quality of His obedience or His devotion to God and Scripture, but we know that there was nothing about Jesus's appearance that called attention to Himself (Isa. 53:2). It surely would have been difficult for Joseph and Mary to bring Him up without being constantly aware of

His miraculous birth—and that this showed in various ways to the other sons. The soil for jealous feelings was ready from the start, and I cannot imagine anybody being any different from these brothers.

They were not even damning Jesus "with faint praise," as the famous playwright John Dryden put it; there was no praise in their words at all! Their caustic remarks were their weapon to make Him look ridiculous—as when the Jews put a robe on Him before Herod (Luke 23:11). They came up with their best language in order to undermine Jesus's ministry. Whereas the truth was, Jesus did only what His heavenly Father wanted and lived solely for the praise that comes from Him only (John 5:19, 44). They accused Jesus of being the diametric opposite to this. Therefore to say "show Yourself to the world—not just here in Nazareth—since You want to be famous in Israel" was designed to cut Him to shreds, to rub His nose in it. It must have hurt. He must have felt it.

His reply to them, however, did not appear to be upset; He did not take the bait but said what was nonetheless to the point: "The right time for me has not yet come; for you any time is right. The world cannot hate you, but it hates me because I testify that what it does is evil. You go to the Feast. I am not yet going up to this Feast, because for me the right time has not yet come" (John 7:6–8). What is interesting is that Jesus did not let on that He knew they were trying to hurt Him. He did not say, "How dare you say I am merely hoping to be a public figure!" It was as if He let them think He agreed with them: "For me the right time has not yet come."

IN THE FACE OF JEALOUSY, KEEP YOUR EYES ON THE FATHER

The lesson Jesus teaches in how to handle another's jealousy is *to overlook it*. He did not say to them, "The trouble with you is that you're just jealous." That would never do. First, it would have been a sin had Jesus done this. Jesus was tempted and yet maintained words, thoughts, and deeds "without sin" (Heb. 4:15). This is why He was so calm and did not lose His temper. He therefore did not sin in His response. Second, He would have stooped to their level had He accused them of being jealous. Third, to accuse another of jealousy never does any good. Fourth, rarely would a jealous person like this admit to jealousy in any case. Finally, Jesus kept His eyes on the Father—and moved on.

They were jealous of Jesus, yes; but was Jesus jealous? No. But was He tempted to be jealous? Yes. Hebrews 4:15 says He was tempted at all points as we are. I am not saying that Jesus was tempted to be jealous of these brothers—probably not. But there would have been other times no doubt when He was tempted to jealousy. Satan tempted Jesus by showing Him "all the kingdoms of the world and their splendor" (Matt. 4:8). That would indicate that Jesus could be tempted to be jealous of those who had everything in this life—compared with His own lifestyle of having no place to lay His head (Luke 9:58). I am only saying that is not unlikely that Jesus was tempted to jealousy; indeed, it is very likely that He was so tempted. In any case, He resisted; this means He never gave in—ever.

Let us never forget that these brothers were later converted. Remember too that the same person who is jealous of you today may be your friend tomorrow. This very possibility should be enough to make you cautious in everything you say at the moment. What you say or don't say could make a huge difference in the situation now—and how you will feel down the road.

Just remember, then, when you read the epistles of James or Jude that these were ordinary men who once felt toward Jesus as every unconverted person initially does. They do not see His glory. They do not see His deity. They do not see that He is the Son of God. They do not see that His death on the cross atoned for our sins (expiation) and turned God's wrath away (propitiation). They do not see that Jesus was raised from the dead. Only the Holy Spirit can reveal these things.

We do not know when Jesus's brothers were converted. Neither do we know how many other brothers there might have been. We do know that Jesus experienced the unpleasantness of sibling rivalry, and we see in this, at least in part, how He handled it. He did not acknowledge it but moved on.

Part III

PARANOID JEALOUSY

Chapter Eight

PERILOUS JEALOUSY

As they danced, they sang: "Saul has slain his thousands, and David his tens of thousands." Saul was very angry; this refrain galled him. "They have credited David with tens of thousands," he thought, "but me with only thousands. What more can he get but the kingdom?" And from that time on Saul kept a jealous eye on David.

—1 SAMUEL 18:7–9

Envy rots the bones.

—PROVERBS 14:30

Jealousy is the injured lover's hell.[1]

—JOHN MILTON

DAVID'S PREPARATION CONSISTED not only in sibling rivalry but also in the painful years of running from King Saul just to stay alive. When Samuel anointed David with oil (1 Sam. 16:13), he did not tell David it would be another twenty years before he actually wore the crown, nor did he tell him the next twenty years would be invaluable preparation for the kingship. I will quote Dr. Martyn Lloyd-Jones again: "The worst thing that can happen to a man is to succeed before he is ready." God was going to make sure that the man after His own heart did not succeed before he was ready. Sibling rivalry may have helped to galvanize David to go after Goliath, but the jealous rivalry King Saul made up in his own paranoid mind actually helped to prepare David for the kingship.

Killing Goliath was in a sense the best thing that had ever happened to David. But it must also be said that it was the worst thing that ever happened to him. It catapulted him to fame in Israel, provided him with a new friendship (with Jonathan, Saul's son), gave him a high rank in Saul's military, and made him immensely popular with all the people, paving the way for him to be king. But it led to more pain than he ever dreamed of. Compliments can do that!

Killing Goliath was the consequence of the anointing that came when Samuel poured oil on him. "From that day on the Spirit of the LORD came upon David in power" (1 Sam. 16:13). That power was manifested in the killing of Goliath.

However, one might wish if only Samuel had said to David, "Oh, by the way, David, I need to tell you: it will be another twenty years before you will wear the crown; until then you will be running from King Saul to save your life—it is part of God's preparation for you." If only.

God's disciplining us seldom comes in advance with a

warning label. He just *does it*, ready or not—whether we like it or not.

KING SAUL

We now embark upon a look at paranoia. Paranoia is a disturbed thought process brought on by excessive anxiety or fear, often to the point of irrationality and delusion. Paranoia is an unfounded or exaggerated distrust in others. The person with paranoia suspects he or she is being followed or being persecuted. Paranoid individuals constantly suspect the trust and motives of those around them and believe that everybody is "out to get them."

Jealousy, then, often accompanies paranoia, and paranoid jealousy is an extreme distrust, even to the point of obsession that someone is disloyal, unfaithful, or that the person you are jealous of wants to destroy you. A king or dictator—even someone in strategic leadership—may imagine that there will be a coup d'état at any moment. The person at the top may not trust those closest to them. It can also enter the home. A husband or wife may think their spouse is cheating on them. It is mostly the consequence of utter insecurity and can almost certainly be traced to a lack of faith in God.

King Saul became insanely jealous of David and, as we will see, was more driven by the fear of David than by threat of the Philistines—Israel's chief enemy. Insecurity can lead a person to have a very unbalanced perspective. Those closest to President Richard Nixon reported that, when he flew to the South Pacific to welcome astronaut Neil Armstrong—the first person to walk on the moon—back home, Nixon was actually more excited over the news that his political rival Edward Kennedy was involved in a scandal than the occasion of greeting Armstrong.

King Saul was now yesterday's man; David was tomorrow's man. Yesterday's man still wore the crown but forfeited the anointing of God's blessing and approval. "I have rejected him as king over Israel," God said to Samuel (1 Sam. 16:1). Indeed, the Lord had "left Saul" (1 Sam. 18:12). On the other hand, David—tomorrow's man—had no crown to wear but was given the blessed anointing of the Spirit of God. So we have this situation: Saul wore the crown without the anointing; David had the anointing without the crown.

It has been said more than once: *if the Holy Spirit were completely withdrawn from the church today, 90 percent of the work of the church would carry on as if nothing had happened.* A Chinese pastor recently visited several churches in the United States. At the end of his tour, having seen so many great churches, he was asked for his impression. The reply: "I am amazed at how much you accomplish without God."

What can happen to the church generally can also happen to an individual; it is when he or she becomes stone deaf to the Holy Spirit and therefore cannot be renewed again to repentance (Heb. 5:12–6:6).

Think about it: King Saul would continue on without the blessing of God—for another twenty years! He still had the power and authority, the prestige, the following, the adulation of the people. *Nobody* knew that Saul was yesterday's man. Except Samuel. And he wasn't telling.

On the other hand, David had the anointing. No platform, no authority, no power, no stature. He could not have known it would be like this for the next twenty years. *Almost nobody* knew that David was tomorrow's man. Samuel knew; David's dad and brothers knew. And David knew. What David didn't know was how long he would have to wait before he would come into his inheritance.

As I quoted above, the worst thing that can happen to a man is to succeed before he is ready. Saul succeeded before he was ready. David, the man after God's own heart, would be preserved and spared the tragedy of succeeding before he was ready.

What would make him ready? Twenty years of *preparation.*

What would God use to prepare him? King Saul's *jealousy.* Has it crossed your mind that God is using other people's jealousy to prepare you? Be of good cheer; you are in good company! It was the chief way God prepared David, a man after His own heart, to be the next king of Israel.

Are you tomorrow's man or woman? Are you waiting for your time to come? Victor Hugo said, "Like the trampling of a mighty army, so is the force of an idea whose time has come." If I might change that slightly: like the trampling of a mighty army, so is the force of one's *anointing* whose time has come. If you are waiting for your time to come, be on the lookout for any kind of preparation God may use. You therefore may be surprised at the manner of preparation God uses.

David was anointed king by Samuel (1 Sam. 16:13), but he would not wear the crown for years and years (2 Sam. 2:10–11). The truth is, David was not ready to be king on the day he was anointed. His anointing needed to be honed, refined, matured, and strengthened. Strange as it may seem, we need more than the anointing.

You too may be tomorrow's man or woman—with an undoubted anointing. But your anointing needs to be nurtured and your gold refined.

The glory David enjoyed from slaying Goliath was short-lived. Praise for what he did came too soon. The women coming out from all the towns of Israel to meet Saul with singing and dancing with their tambourines and lutes sounded lovely—at first: "Saul has slain his thousands, and *David his tens of thousands*" (1 Sam. 18:7, emphasis added).

Oh, dear. This is not good. The women could not have known how insensitive they were to a king's huge ego. Most people have no idea how big their hero's ego actually sometimes is and how insecure he truly may be. So many of us in ministry have a few admirers, but our followers have us on a pedestal—a thing we should not knowingly allow. They think we are so secure and godly and have no need of a compliment. They don't realize that when we finish preaching we ask ourselves, "Did I do OK?" We dare not admit these are our thoughts. But they *are* our thoughts. They are certainly mine.

I used to have people come to me after the Sunday *night* service and say, "I loved your sermon this *morning*." They could not have known that it was the one I just preached I'd love feedback on; I had forgotten about the one earlier in the day. I begin to think, "They liked this morning's sermon, but not tonight's." Yes, I had thoughts like that all the time.

I am therefore a little bit sympathetic with Saul. I think I too would have immediately noticed that, had I been Saul, they praised David more than me.

The question is: what should you do when jealousy first sets in? I answer: you go to your knees. You pour out your complaint to the Lord. You confess your weakness and insecurity. Don't cover it up, don't justify it, and don't sweep it under the carpet. You say to God, "Lord, I am so sorry I feel this way. Thank You for accepting me. Thank You for remembering that I am dust. Thank You, Lord Jesus, for being touched with the feeling of my weaknesses and not moralizing me."

That is what Saul should have done.

The problem was, Saul had already blown it by deliberately rejecting the biblical injunction regarding offering burnt offerings. He took himself too seriously by taking Samuel's place when he said, "Bring *me* the burnt offering and the fellowship offerings" (1 Sam. 13:9). Big mistake. Fatal mistake. (He went right against the injunctions in the Mosaic Law about people not ordained to the priesthood offering such offerings.) It is what precipitated his downfall. "You acted foolishly," said Samuel, who proceeded to tell Saul his kingdom would not endure and that God had sought out a man after His own heart (vv. 13–14).

In other words, by his disobedience King Saul had already set himself up to let jealousy rule him. He knew that young David was the very person Samuel had referred to. Instead of bowing to Samuel's word and honoring David, Saul dug in his heels—and spent the next twenty years of his life trying to destroy David.

When our ways do not please the Lord, we become perilously vulnerable to letting jealousy set in and grow.

For this reason, the moment we feel a jealous spirit working its way into our hearts, we should fall on our faces and pray as I suggested above.

Do not play around with jealousy. Don't deny it. Admit to it. Perhaps you should tell one other person—get them to pray with you. But if you do not nip jealousy in the bud, its end will be a destruction you don't want to contemplate.

I don't want to give anybody a guilt trip, however. We all have problems with jealousy. Do not say to yourself, "I must be yesterday's man," "I must be yesterday's woman," merely because you have jealous feelings. We all have these thoughts. All the time.

But at the same time I would lovingly urge you to confess your feelings to God at once, lest they get out of hand. Don't repress; that is, don't live in denial.

How does jealousy grow? *Jealousy leads to fear.* "Saul was afraid of David, because the LORD was with David but had left

Saul" (1 Sam. 18:12). That fear, which comes not from God but from below (James 3:14–15), will blind you, warp your sense of integrity, take away the ability to think clearly, pervert your perspective, and even cause you to lose common sense.

Instead of dealing with his jealousy, Saul tried to kill David. The very next day after hearing the women praising David more than Saul, he hurled a spear at David, saying to himself, "I'll pin him to the wall" (1 Sam. 18:10–11). David eluded him twice. But that was only the beginning.

What a shock it must have been for David to discover God's manner of preparation for him! Saul, who had been David's hero, was now his enemy. Those who lead nations often experience extremes of emotions. One of the most unforgettable moments for me in recent British history was when Prime Minister Margaret Thatcher suffered a coup d'état by those whom she thought were her friends. They brought her government down overnight. "It's a funny old world," Margaret Thatcher said shortly after this historic event. David would have agreed.

Think about it—I will say it again: Saul became so possessed with getting rid of David that he was more preoccupied with young David than he was with Israel's archenemy, the Philistines. That is an example of how our perspective can be distorted if we do not cope with jealousy in a godly manner.

Therefore part of our preparation is sometimes having to learn how to cope with another person's jealousy of us. How you respond can be crucial. You will need a lot of prayer, a lot of patience, a loving spirit, and a lot of wisdom. How was David himself doing? "David behaved himself wisely in all his ways; and the LORD was with him" (1 Sam. 18:14, KJV).

Once jealousy degenerates to fear, there is no end to the depth of corruption one may enter into. King Saul even swore an oath to his son Jonathan that he would not kill David, once Jonathan pleaded with his father. "As surely as the LORD lives, David will not be put to death," Saul swore to his own son (1 Sam. 19:6). In ancient times, the swearing of an oath was the *one sure way* another knew you were telling the truth and you would keep your word. A promise is one thing, but if you swore an *oath*, it put "an end to all argument" (Heb. 6:16). But King Saul even broke his oath—to his son Jonathan! Saul immediately tried to kill David (1 Sam. 19:9–10).

But Saul sunk to depths even lower than that. Saul even tried to kill his son Jonathan (1 Sam. 20:33).

Although you may have difficulty accepting this, the Spirit of God actually came upon Saul during this time. Saul had been given the gift of prophecy (1 Sam. 10:9–11). This gift apparently stayed with him, despite his disobedience and God withdrawing His approval of him as stated in 1 Samuel 18:12. While Saul was chasing David toward Naioth, "the Spirit of God came even upon him [Saul], and he walked along prophesying until he came to Naioth" (1 Sam. 19:23). Had David known about this, I wonder how that would have made him feel. To think that David had been anointed by Samuel to be the next king was one thing, but the Spirit of God also coming on his enemy

Saul—whom God rejected—was another! How David would have felt, we can only guess. My guess is, he would have felt perplexed. How could the very same Spirit of God who came on him (1 Sam. 16:13) also come upon his enemy Saul (1 Sam. 19:23)—whom God had deserted?

Figure that one out. My answer: the gifts and calling of God are "irrevocable" ("without repentance," Rom. 11:29, KJV). That means that you get to keep your gift, even if you don't walk with the Lord. But it also means that having a gift of the Spirit (as in 1 Corinthians 12:8–10) is no sure sign of God's anointed blessing and approval. It only means that your gift may function from time to time, as it did with the famous TV evangelists in the 1980s—and with some high-profile fallen leaders in recent years. People ask: how could God use a person while he is simultaneously living in sin? I answer: Romans 11:29.

And yet to think that God could send His Spirit upon one's *enemy* is not too easy to take in! To think that the Spirit of God falls on the very person you know God has negated is difficult to grasp. God's ways are higher than our ways (Isa. 55:8–9). But it does help explain how God will use people who are gifted but not pleasing to the Lord in other ways.

We must not feel betrayed by the Lord if God blesses our enemy. The psalmist admits that he "envied the arrogant" when he saw the prosperity of the wicked (Ps. 73:3), that is, "till I entered the sanctuary of God; then I understood their final destiny" (v. 17).

There was nothing David did—or could do—that changed Saul's mind. Nothing. Had Saul a sense of integrity he would have called off his search for David long before, but especially after he saw how David had a chance to get even—but didn't. When David had a chance to kill Saul, he settled for cutting off a corner of Saul's robe. He pointed out to King Saul how he could have killed him. "Some urged me to kill you, but I spared you.... Now understand and recognize that I am not guilty of wrongdoing or rebellion" (1 Sam. 24:10–11). Saul wept aloud when he saw what David could have done (v. 16). Saul even admitted that David would be king one day (v. 20).

But it did not stop Saul from his continued pursuit of David. He kept coming after David, and David had yet another chance to get vengeance upon Saul, but he refused. David said to Abishai, who volunteered to kill Saul, "Don't destroy him! Who can lay a hand on the LORD's anointed and be guiltless?... The LORD himself will strike him; either his time will come and he will die, or he will go into battle and perish. But the LORD forbid that I should lay a hand on the LORD's anointed. Now get the spear and water jug that are near his head, and let's go" (1 Sam. 26:9–11).

All this was part of David's preparation. He was being tested to the hilt—to see how he would respond. Question: how are you responding when people are jealous of you? How you respond will determine how far away you are from being used of God. If you exploit your opportunity for vindication, it could be a bad sign; God will need to test you a while longer. But if you resist the temptation to get a quick vindication, it is a good sign; God's plans for you may be fulfilled soon.

When jealousy in our own hearts is not dealt with, then, it will know no bounds of wickedness and evil. Saul even sought the witch of Endor after having banned mediums and spiritists from the land. Saul finally admitted that he had sinned. "I have sinned.... Surely I have acted like a fool and have erred greatly" (1 Sam. 26:21). Saul confessed in the end, just before committing suicide, "God has turned away from me. He no longer answers me, either by prophets or by dreams" (1 Sam. 28:15). These are among the saddest words in the Bible.

A jealous spirit will keep you from hearing God. This is perhaps the worst thing of all about jealousy. It breeds deafness. The writer of Hebrews warned the Hebrew Christians about their becoming hard of hearing (Heb. 5:11, kjv). The warning, "Today, if you hear his voice" (Heb. 3:15; Ps. 95:7), was appropriate to these Hebrew Christians because the worst scenario was to be unable to be renewed to repentance (Heb. 6:4–6)—because of stone deafness, the utter inability to hear God anymore. That is what eventually happened to King Saul.

Saul's life ended, then, by Saul taking his own life (1 Sam. 31:4). And yet, although it was a case of Saul's committing suicide, God Himself took the responsibility. "Saul died because he was unfaithful to the Lord; he did not keep the word of the Lord.... So the Lord put him to death" (1 Chron. 10:13–14). Or as the prophet put it: "So in my anger I gave you a king, and in my wrath I took him away" (Hos. 13:11). What is more, Saul succeeded before he was ready.

Those were not easy days for David. But God was developing him into a solid man of God, one who would have true inner dignity, stature, integrity, and ability to hear God speak. When he tried to cut off a corner of Saul's robe, he was "conscience-stricken for having cut off a corner of his robe" (1 Sam. 24:5). That seems a harmless, almost playful thing to do, but not to David. He was *so* sorry he had done that. Why? God was teaching David His *ways*. God said of ancient Israel, "They have not known my ways" (Ps. 95:10). God wants you and me to know His "ways." One of His ways is that His Holy Spirit is easily grieved. The third person of the Trinity, the Holy Spirit, is a very, very sensitive person. I wanted to call my book *The Sensitivity of the Spirit* the "Hypersensitivity of the Spirit," but people talked me out of it—convincing me that the title would be misunderstood, and I am sure they were right. But I still make that very point in my book. When Paul said, "Do not grieve the Holy Spirit of God, with whom you were sealed for the day of redemption" (Eph. 4:30), he used a Greek word that means "to get your feelings hurt." The Holy Spirit can get His feelings hurt. And the Holy Spirit that was resident in David was "hurt" when David tried to cut off a corner of Saul's robe. That is why David was "conscience-stricken." God was teaching David His "ways."

Therefore Saul's jealousy was not for nothing. Not only was

all that was going on letting Saul fill out his folly, but Saul was also an instrument of God's Spirit to refine David.

When people are jealous of you, ask yourself: what is God up to in letting them feel as they do? If you react negatively, you will never know what God might have done in your life. But if you react as David did, and do nothing to cut down your enemy but wait on God's time to exalt you, who knows, you may be a head of state one day! His preparation is part of His design, lest you succeed before you are ready.

Chapter Nine

JEALOUS OFFSPRING

Anger is cruel and fury overwhelming, but who can stand before jealousy?

—PROVERBS 27:4

A wise son brings joy to his father.

—PROVERBS 15:20

A foolish son brings grief to his father.

—PROVERBS 17:25

MY FATHER USED to quote the proverb—"A wise son brings joy to his father"—as I grew up. Whether this added to the pressure I was already under to be a good son, who knows? I only know I have been fairly consumed with the need to have my dad's approval.

Some readers may remember watching President George W. Bush on television when he addressed the nation from a church immediately following the events of September 11, 2001. When he sat down, two seats away from his father, former President George H. W. Bush, the latter reached over and patted his son on the knee, showing obvious paternal approval. I have wondered many times since how often the younger Bush may have brought joy to his father.

The rivalry between father and son is a delicate subject. Perhaps even more sensitive is the matter of jealousy that sometimes exists between mother and daughter. The mother can be threatened if her daughter is more beautiful, talented, and sexy; the daughter can be threatened if she is nowhere as attractive as her mother, especially if the mother continues to look young—or tries to look young. The kind of rivalry that can exists between father and son usually relates to achievement. I did not grow up with a problem in this area as far as I can tell; my dad only wanted me to succeed—and outdo him. But this was not too hard to do, seeing that he was relatively uneducated—never going to college or university and working most of his life as a low-paying clerk for the Chesapeake and Ohio Railway Company. He was not an ambitious man. He lived for his church and, if anything, lived his life through me, hoping I would achieve what he never did—becoming a preacher. But there was never any rivalry between us.

This chapter however is relevant not merely for family rivalry. It touches on one of the most common occurrences throughout the church and the world: that of the successor determining to outdo his or her predecessor. It can refer to a physician, a businessman, any professional person, a pastor, vicar, bishop, archbishop—even the pope! I am sure that Pope Benedict XVI must get used to being compared all the time to John Paul II, arguably the most popular pope of all time. Worship leaders, ministers of music, and teachers face the same thing—being compared to the previous person in the same position. Pastors' wives face this too.

Mrs. Martyn Lloyd-Jones did me an enormous favor one day when I was having a cup of tea with her. She knew of the criticisms I was getting and the pressure I was under at Westminster Chapel, having followed her husband—probably the greatest preacher of the twentieth century. She knew how people would say of me, "RT is OK, but he is no Martyn Lloyd-Jones." So she said to me that day, "You are only going through the same thing Martyn went through. He would get so annoyed when people would say, 'Dr. Lloyd-Jones is good, but he's no Campbell Morgan.'" How sweet of her to say this to me. I have passed this story on to my successor at the chapel now, Rev. Greg Haslam. "Comparisons are onerous," said William Shakespeare.

I have always been surprised that David left a huge gap in his leadership regarding the timing and appointment of his successor. It is clear to the readers of the Bible who the successor was to be—Solomon—but apparently this was not always so clear to everybody living at the time. Or perhaps David simply did not want to give up power while he was alive. He may have assumed that his death would be followed by a smooth transition. However, David, not the greatest father of all time, should have anticipated a rivalry among his sons, but he seemingly didn't. One of them—Absalom—couldn't wait for his father to die; he decided to get the job while David was still in power. If indeed Absalom knew that the next king was supposed to be Solomon, he found a shrewd way to secure the kingship while David was still alive.

ABSALOM

"If only I were appointed judge in the land! Then everyone who has a complaint or case could come to me and I would see that he gets justice."...So he [Absalom] stole the hearts of the men of Israel.

—2 SAMUEL 15:4, 6

King David was Israel's greatest king, but, as I said, he certainly wasn't perfect. All his preparation during Saul's lifetime got him ready for the kingship, but it did not anticipate everything David could face. For one thing, it did not preserve him from sexual temptation. David sinned by committing adultery with Bathsheba and then sinned more heinously by trying to cover up his adultery by killing Uriah, Bathsheba's husband. David seemed to have gotten away with it for a couple of years, until the prophet Nathan uncovered the whole thing and David's life fell apart.

"You may be sure that your sin will find you out," said Moses (Num. 32:23). But David took a chance that maybe that word might not apply to him—since he was king and also a man after God's own heart. Wrong. God is no respecter of persons. And whom the Lord *loves*, He disciplines (Heb. 12:6). Chastening is not tit for tat or God getting even, and yet sometimes it is required that we must face up to our folly—lest we bring God's name into disrepute. Because God loved David and had more to teach him, He sent the prophet Nathan to expose his sin.

Perhaps the most ominous part of Nathan's prophecy was this: "The sword will never depart from your house" (2 Sam. 12:10).

I must divert for a moment to relate this story. I preached on the life of David for two years when I was at Westminster Chapel. But at the end of eighteen months, having just finished my exposition of 2 Samuel 12—when Nathan gives the afore-mentioned prophecy, I decided to suspend, or close down, the series altogether. "Why?" asked the deacons. "Because the rest of the life of David is so sad, I simply cannot bear to take us through it all." The men seemingly accepted my verdict but did not seem thrilled.

As it happened, our church had a day of prayer and fasting during this time. Something happened that day that was rare for me. It was *almost* as if I heard God speak in clear words: "So you aren't going to finish your series on David. Don't you know that is where most of your people are?"—meaning that they too were like David. "They have sinned and have had to cope with a guilty past and a bleak future." I was shocked. I returned to the series the following Sunday, and I can tell you, the last part of David's life—"the downside"—turned out to be the best part of the entire series. People seemed to be blessed to no end.

But now to the "downside" of David's life. Soon after Nathan's prophetic word, David's son Amnon raped his sister Tamar (2 Sam. 13:1–14). Absalom waited awhile but then killed his brother Amnon to get revenge for disgracing their sister. This forced Absalom to live in exile for a while. Absalom became very resentful and jealous of his father during this time and also became envious for the kingship. After he was finally reunited with his father, King David, Absalom conspired to take the throne. David had apparently lost touch with the people; Absalom found a way to win their hearts—and did so. He listened carefully to the people's complaints so that he "stole the hearts of the men of Israel" (2 Sam. 15:6). At the appropriate time he managed to get the people to shout, "Absalom is king in Hebron." He even won over the respected Ahithophel, known for his unusual wisdom, in the process. When David was told "the hearts of the men of Israel are with Absalom," David gave in and went into exile (vv. 13–18). It is one of the saddest moments in the Old Testament.

When Jealousy Triumphs Over You

What emerges is a rare lesson in how to cope when your jealous enemy has prevailed over you. This kind of thing happens all the time, and it happened to David. His twenty years of preparation may not have kept him from sexual sin, but it certainly prepared him for this era—one of the worst of his whole life. Although the sword was now cutting into his household right, left, and center, there is one thing David had throughout: presence of mind.

The same David who behaved wisely in all his ways when coping with Saul's jealousy now did it again—coping in the fallout of his own son's jealousy. Who would normally be prepared for such a challenge? But David apparently was. David did not put a foot wrong—and he did so without the counsel of Ahithophel, whose advice "was like that of one who inquires of God" (2 Sam. 16:23). It is one thing to have good counsel around you; it is quite another when you are alone—and don't even have a priest or prophet. Here is how David overcame his son's jealousy.

1. David did not fight back.

"We must leave [Jerusalem] immediately"—and he did (2 Sam. 15:14–17). He was being a type of Christ and living what Jesus would later teach. Jesus said, "Do not resist an evil person. If someone strikes you on the right cheek, turn to him the other also. And if someone wants to sue you and take your tunic, let him have your cloak as well. If someone forces you to go one mile, go with him two miles" (Matt. 5:39–41). David might have gotten his army grouped—and destroyed Absalom—but he felt that Nathan's prophecy was now being further unfolded. David was not going to lift a finger to overturn it. "The king set out, with his entire household following him" (2 Sam. 15:16).

2. David did not try to amass a huge following.

He only allowed Ittai the Gittite to stay with him after Ittai pleaded to stay. "Why should you come along with us? Go back and stay with King Absalom....Go back, and take your countrymen. May kindness and faithfulness be with you." Ittai insisted and stayed with David. "The whole countryside wept aloud as all the people passed by" (2 Sam. 15:19–23).

3. David was utterly, totally, and unreservedly resigned to the sovereign will of God.

David would not manipulate God to get the kingship back. To prove it, he told Zadok the priest, "Take the ark of God back into the city. If I find favor in the LORD's eyes, he will bring me back and let me see it and his dwelling place again. But if he says, 'I am not pleased with you' then I am ready; let him do to me whatever seems good to him" (2 Sam. 15:25–26). I find this extraordinary. This was David's opportunity to have the most sacred, revered, and cherished item in Israel—the ark of God, which symbolized the very presence of God. David might have even felt more secure with the ark nearby. But no. He refused to take it with him.

4. David relied on prayer in his most desperate moment.

Having been told, "Ahithophel is among the conspirators with Absalom," David prayed, "O LORD, turn Ahithophel's counsel into foolishness" (2 Sam. 15:31). That was the only weapon he had up to that moment—prayer. This reveals the true heart of David. It shows why he was called a man after God's own heart. What do you do when all have forsaken you, when all good counsel seems gone, when the outlook is bleak, when you feel that God's judgment is behind all that is going on and when you are deplete of wisdom? You pray. That's all. You pray. That is what David did.

5. David recognized how God might be answering his prayer.

He suddenly and providentially ran into Hushai the Arkite. David had not expected this. But under his nose, right after praying as he did, God sent a link by which David's prayer would be answered. His prayer was, "Turn Ahithophel's counsel into foolishness." Then Hushai shows up—who had access to "king" Absalom. David acted wisely; he told Hushai to return to Jerusalem to be available to counter Ahithophel's advice. The same God who predestines the end equally predestines the *means to the end*. David felt that Hushai's sudden turning up after praying as he did was an immediate answer to prayer (2 Sam. 15:32–37).

6. David manifested a meek spirit and would not retort.

When he was attacked by Shimei, son of Gera, who cursed David and accused him of getting what he deserved, David refused to fight back. Instead he said, "It may be that the LORD will see my distress and repay me with good for the cursing I am receiving today" (2 Sam. 16:12). It was said of Jesus, "When they hurled insults at him, he did not retaliate; when he suffered, he made no threats. Instead, he entrusted himself to him who judges justly" (1 Pet. 2:23). Keep in mind: David knew all that was going on was from God's hand. Why should he fight it? He had the same spirit of resignation as did Job: "The LORD gave and the LORD has taken away; may the name of the LORD be praised" (Job 1:21).

7. David wanted his enemy to be preserved and spared.

He ordered his men to "be gentle" with Absalom whenever they ran into him (2 Sam. 18:5). Although Absalom had sadly become his father's enemy, David's heart was mellow toward him. David knew in his heart that God wasn't finished with him and that he would return to his throne. His concern was for Absalom, hoping to win his love. This is the way we should be with all our enemies. I want my enemy to say to me, "You were brilliant with me the whole time." Today's enemy may be tomorrow's friend. They will remember what you were like in the heat of the battle. Love them now; they may love you later.

David was simply determined to let God fight this battle.

In a word: David took God's prerogative seriously: "It is mine to avenge; I will repay. In due time their foot will slip" (Deut. 32:35). In other words, David was utterly dedicated to letting God vindicate him. That is the way he coped with King Saul's jealousy; that is the way he coped with Absalom's jealousy. "For the LORD God is a sun and shield; the LORD bestows favor and honor; no good thing does he withhold from those whose walk is blameless" (Ps. 84:11).

Sadly, Absalom was the polar opposite to his father. The true character of Absalom is seen in that "during his lifetime Absalom had taken a pillar and erected it in the King's Valley as a monument to himself.... He named the pillar after himself, and it is called Absalom's Monument to this day" (2 Sam. 18:18). The untold truth of your jealous enemy will emerge in due time. "The sins of some men are obvious; reaching the place of judgment ahead of them; the sins of others trail behind them" (1 Tim. 5:24).

It broke David's heart when his son met his death. "O my son Absalom! My son, my son Absalom! If only I had died instead of you—O Absalom, my son, my son!" (2 Sam. 18:33). Vindication came, but it was far from sweet.

ADONIJAH

> King David was old and well advanced in years.... Now Adonijah, whose mother was Haggith, put himself forward and said, "I will be king."
>
> —1 KINGS 1:1, 5

David had several wives and several sons. So far not one of them would give him "joy" by their wisdom but rather "grief" by their folly. Up to now he apparently sired vain, ambitious, and envious men—jealous of their father and each other. Adonijah was born "next after Absalom" (1 Kings 1:6) and showed his utter lack of wisdom by repeating his brother's folly.

By this time Adonijah certainly knew who the successor to David should be—Solomon. The proof: who was invited and who was not invited to the coronation. The dead giveaway that Adonijah knew who the successor should be was by his not inviting Zadok the priest or Nathan the prophet—or Solomon himself (1 Kings 1:7–10). And yet the ultimate blame for all this falls on the lap of David. "His father had never interfered with him [Adonijah] by asking, 'Why do you behave as you do?'"

(v. 6). The writer of the Book of 1 Kings thus infers that David himself should have anticipated and avoided a crisis like this.

It took the bold intervention of Nathan the prophet and David's wife Bathsheba to persuade the ailing King David to appoint Solomon immediately and to stop Adonijah from being crowned king—at the last minute (1 Kings 1:11–38). Thus God overruled at the end of the day. As Job learned, no plan of God can be "thwarted" (Job 42:2). Remember this when jealous men seem to be having their way.

Solomon would have indeed brought joy to his father by his wisdom. His initial wisdom was asking God for wisdom when he could have asked for anything (1 Kings 3:5–15). God gave Solomon extraordinary wisdom and very great insight, making him "wiser than any other man" (1 Kings 4:31). Except for one thing: Solomon loved many foreign women, was not fully devoted to the Lord in the end as David had been, and did evil in the eyes of the Lord (1 Kings 11:1–6). I have often been amazed that a man with such wisdom could at the same time be so stupid. But the greatest of earthly wisdom has its blind spots. The best of men are men at best. God vowed to "tear the kingdom" away from Solomon (v. 11). The first sign this was coming was through his insecure and jealous offspring Rehoboam.

REHOBOAM

My little finger is thicker than my father's waist. My father laid on you a heavy yoke; I will make it even heavier. My father scourged you with whips; I will scourge you with scorpions.

—1 KINGS 12:10–11

In my Bible reading plan, which I follow every year, I always dread coming to 1 Kings 12. I cringe as I read. It is *so* painful. I think to myself, "Oh, no, how could he do this?" It is so sad. But, like it or not, there is a need in all of us to outdo in some way those who went before us. And yet if we carefully guard that need, God will use us. But if, unwisely, we try to play "one-upmanship" with those who precede us, we will be seen as complete fools.

Presidents do this. Doctors and lawyers do this. Ministers do this. Scientists do this. There is a need to show who is stronger and better.

Mind you, Rehoboam had a pretty hard act to follow. All the world came to hear Solomon's wisdom and to see the gold and finery for which he was famous. During his reign there was peace, prosperity, security—everything. Except that Solomon's heart had grown cold toward the Lord.

If only Rehoboam had seized on *that*. The kings that were great after Solomon's day—such as Hezekiah and Josiah—had one thing in common: their love for God and His Word and getting it right according to Scripture. Nothing else. You were not required to be a genius like Solomon or a military leader like David. The fear of God would do it! Rehoboam might have been even greater than Solomon had he put God first!

Nothing could be more foolish than to try to upstage a man

147

like Solomon. But Rehoboam was a small man. Moreover, his very installation meant that judgment upon Israel had begun. A small man in power who is not motivated by the fear of God is often a sign already that God is displeased with that nation. A mere claim to love God—when it happens to be politically correct—is not enough. When one is motivated by jealousy to outdo one's father, it is not a sign of wonderful things to come. Rather the opposite, as it turned out to be regarding the kingship of Rehoboam. "My little finger is thicker than my father's waist" (1 Kings 12:10). What an arrogant—and untruthful—thing his friends advised him to say.

It is a very small man who needs to prove himself by such a statement. It was all talk. All Israel knew in one stroke that they had trouble coming and that it was an end to a golden era: "To your tents, O Israel! Look after your own house, O David!" (v. 16).

You see it in churches. The new pastor or vicar so often needs to prove how much better he is than the previous leader. He changes things overnight. He does everything differently. He makes comments and innuendos that indicate the former regime is happily over and that good things at last are coming. "My father laid on you a heavy yoke; I will make it even heavier." The previous man did it one way; here is the way we do it now.

It is so often all down to the insecurity of the new man, the need to prove oneself, the hope that people will respect the new man and forget the old.

Here is what Rehoboam should have done. Knowing that

he could not even begin to compete with his father's wisdom, power, and glory, he should have extolled his father to the hilt and sought the honor that God alone would have given to just Rehoboam (John 5:44). Kings who humbled themselves, even the wicked Ahab, managed to stave off the just wrath of God when they repented. (See 1 Kings 21:29.) Rehoboam need not have been the vehicle of God's judgment. He could have postponed judgment and continued the happy era. He could have truly *upstaged* his father! How? By *not* loving foreign women and by adhering to all of the mandates in the Mosaic Law, thus experiencing precisely what God would have done for *him*. God has a plan for each of us, and the fulfillment of that plan—even if it does not mean we will be as great and glorious as the one we followed—will be utterly *satisfying*.

But Rehoboam instead allowed Judah to set up "high places, sacred stones and Asherah poles on every high hill and under every spreading tree. There were even male shrine prostitutes in the land; the people engaged in all the detestable practices of the nations the LORD had driven out before the Israelites" (1 Kings 14:23–24). In Solomon's day there was gold, gold, gold—everywhere. Everything seemed to be of gold. They had gold running out of their ears! But Rehoboam, who boasted that he was tougher than his father, in only the fifth year of his reign helplessly watched Shishak king of Egypt attack Jerusalem and carry off the treasures of the temple and the royal palace. Shishak took everything, "including all the gold shields Solomon had made" (v. 26). Rehoboam "made bronze shields to replace them" (v. 27). Bronze. What a price to pay because one is governed by sheer jealousy.

We saw at the beginning of this book that envy can be productive (Eccles. 4:4). But it is counterproductive jealousy—like that which controlled Rehoboam—that made him want to compare himself to Solomon as he did and then try to outdo his legendary father. Being the best that ever was is not God's desire for any of us! Give up on that! Put in its place a burning desire to receive the honor, glory, praise, and approval that *comes from God only* (John 5:44)—and that will be more than enough to satisfy you. I guarantee it.

But jealousy is an awful thing. It transcends culture, blood relationships, intellectual gifting, parental pressures, religious background, education, socioeconomic class, and your job. If you let it control you, it will damn you. If you control it, it will lie beneath your feet.

Let God exalt you, let Him fight your battles, and let Him vindicate you—no matter how long it takes. If you do this, you will know the wisdom of Proverbs, the joy of the Lord, the peace that passes knowledge, and the immediate presence of the Holy Spirit.

Chapter Ten

FATAL JEALOUSY

After Jesus was born in Bethlehem in Judea, during
the time of King Herod, Magi from the east came
to Jerusalem and asked, "Where is the one who
has been born king of the Jews? We saw his star
in the east and have come to worship him." When
King Herod heard this he was disturbed, and all
Jerusalem with him.

—MATTHEW 2:1–3

O jealousy, thou ugliest fiend of hell![1]

—HANNAH MORE

O UR STUDY OF royal rivals continues. The focus in
this chapter is on the Herods. The era of the Herods
paralleled the first great awakening, a period beginning with the birth of Jesus and continuing through the period
described in the Acts of the Apostles. The Herods were from
a Jewish family of Idumean descent (from the Edomites), and
they were never fully accepted by the Jews. The first Herod (c.
37–4 B.C.), also known as Herod the Great, rebuilt the temple

151

at Jerusalem. Solomon built the first temple; the second was built after the Babylonian exile. Although Herod's temple was literally the third temple that had been erected on the holy site, the Jews (to this day) call it the Second Temple, as if to show contempt for Herod's temple. Herod worked for the Roman authorities and was given the title "King of the Jews"—not by the Jews but by the Roman authorities in 37 B.C. Herod probably never felt safe with that title, knowing as he did that the Jews regarded him with disdain. Therefore the notion of a rival "king of the Jews" being born somewhere would cause his insecurity to surface like nothing else.

This chapter is thus an extension of our study of paranoid jealousy, only that it ends even more horrendously than in previous cases. For example, whereas King Saul's life ended in his committing suicide, King Herod the Great ended up destroying countless male babies in and around ancient Bethlehem (Matt. 2:16).

The Great Awakening

It all began with a sudden awakening of God—a phenomenon for which nobody was prepared—first manifested through an unexpected group of unusual people, called the Magi. Nothing would be more threatening to a secular king in a nation with a godly heritage than an authentic awakening by the Spirit of God. It brought jealousy to a level of decadence, paranoia, and fear that exceeded anything we have seen yet. I suspect that a true awakening from God could have a similar effect on the leadership of any nation that has a history of revering the God of the Bible.

My wife, Louise, and I have made the journey to Enfield, Connecticut, twice in recent years—just to pray at the spot where Jonathan Edwards preached his epoch-making sermon "Sinners in the Hands of an Angry God." There is nothing sacred about that spot in Enfield; praying there is no more efficacious than praying in Israel or Tennessee. But I have wanted to do this for these reasons: to try to feel what it must have been like on that occasion and also to ask God to do it again. I have even asked that a measure of Jonathan Edwards's mantle would fall on me, that I could preach like that. God has not answered that prayer.

Edwards's famous sermon was preached on July 8, 1741. (I just noticed that today as I write is July 8, 2008—Edwards preached this 267 years ago today.) Taking his text from Deuteronomy 32:35—"their foot shall slide in due time" (KJV)—Edwards spoke on the reality of hell and eternal punishment. It is said that, immediately following the sermon, strong men held on to the church pews inside the building and to tree trunks outside to keep from sliding into hell, so great was the power of the Spirit on the hearers. This sermon came at the high watermark of the Great Awakening in New England, a period that lasted roughly from 1725 to 1750. It is what gave America its Bible belt.

The difference between revival and a great awakening is that the former affects only the church—reviving and empowering it. A great awakening is more than revival; it impacts the world, government, and society outside the church. Even culture. Politics. Secular institutions. We must pray for revival, yes, but what is needed at the present time is that which will affect the entire world. I fear that no movement of the Holy Spirit has done that for a long time.

King Herod (the Great)

The first great awakening took place at about the same time as the birth of Jesus. It was when the Magi (sometimes called the three wise men) came from the east, following a star, which they believe was leading them to the king of the Jews. They could not have known that their visit to Jerusalem aroused the jealousy and insecurity of King Herod. He was "disturbed" ("troubled"—Matt. 2:3, kjv). He was scared to death. The thought of the birth of a rival royal is the sort of thing he would fear most and yet something for which he was not prepared.

A true awakening of the Holy Spirit is always likely to do this sort of thing—arouse jealousy—in those who occupy highest places of leadership. Some leaders, even church leaders, are fearful of a deep awakening of the Holy Spirit because it competes with their sense of control. Leaders are happy for a movement of the Spirit as long as they themselves can be in control. But to have the Holy Spirit take control is very threatening indeed. Could it be that if leaders in strategic places were willing to surrender control, the Spirit of God would come sooner rather than later? For one thing, we have to let God use people whom we would not normally welcome!

People, especially some of the clergy, were jealous of Jonathan Edwards during the time of the Great Awakening—and afterward. They were jealous of Evan Roberts in the aftermath of the Welsh Revival (1904–1905). When God gives you a special anointing, expect jealousy; it goes with the territory.

God sometimes chooses people who naturally make others jealous. He uses people who "get our goat"! They may be uneducated, uncultured, foreign, or outside our comfort zone. As I said in *Out of the Comfort Zone*, God likes to choose people and do things through them that make sophisticated people to say, "Yuck!" He offends the mind to reveal the heart.

Unexpected people often appear out of the blue when God works powerfully. In the case of the time of King Herod, the "Magi" showed up. Nobody had invited them; nobody expected them; nobody knew anything about them. They just came. Revival often comes like this—when no one really expects it.

When God is powerfully at work, moreover, people will come from everywhere. There will be no need to advertise, no need to make an effort to get the word out. I am not being critical of advertising; I am only saying that when there is a very high level or great measure of the Holy Spirit at work, our efforts to get a crowd will be unnecessary. "Those who are far away will come and help to build the temple of the LORD" (Zech. 6:15). "I revealed myself to those who did not ask for me; I was found by those who did not seek me. To a nation that did not call on my name, I said, 'Here am I, here am I'" (Isa. 65:1). "'Come, see a man who told me everything I ever did. Could this be the

Christ?' They came out of the town and made their way toward him" (John 4:29–30).

Jesus said, "I sent you to reap what you have not worked for. Others have done the hard work, and you have reaped the benefits of their labor" (John 4:38).

The Magi had no idea that their question, "Where is the one who has been born king of the Jews? We saw his star in the east" (Matt. 2:2), would cause a stir. They assumed that not only had the child been born already but also that everybody would know exactly where to find Him! Wow. Were they ever wrong! They pushed a hot button with a mere question to which they thought there was a quick answer!

A great awakening will stir the ordinary, grassroots people. "The common people heard him gladly" (Mark 12:37, KJV). But this sort of thing stirs up the jealousy of those who have been in power. We may wish we could always touch the "high and mighty"—the people of influence. But that is the wrong way around. We must be willing to start at the bottom. It is typical that a fresh work of God begins with the most ordinary people—like The Salvation Army and the Pentecostal and holiness movements.

The first great awakening got people to reading their Bibles! Herod asked the chief priests and teachers of the law where the Christ was to be born. The reply: in Bethlehem, for it is written: "But you, Bethlehem, in the land of Judah, are by no means least among the rulers of Judah; for out of you will come a ruler who will be the shepherd of my people Israel" (Matt. 2:6; see also Micah 5:2). A true awakening of the Holy Spirit will result in a return to the Bible. You can count on that. Any so-called awakening or revival that does not drive people to the Word of God is a counterfeit movement.

However, unwarranted professions will accompany a true move of God. Sadly, there will always be those who profess but don't possess the real faith. King Herod ordered the Magi to make a careful search for the new king of the Jews, "so that I too may go and worship him" (Matt. 2:8). That was a lie. He would do the opposite. But in the midst of a true work of the Spirit, do not expect that all who claim to be interested in spiritual things really are. It will be a time when people get on the bandwagon; they will do what is "politically correct," as when American politicians all claim to be born again.

In the meantime, the wicked Herod, realizing that the Magi would not report back to him, "gave orders to kill all the boys in Bethlehem and its vicinity who were two years old and under, in accordance with the time he had learned from the Magi" (Matt. 2:16). This fulfilled the prophecy of Jeremiah: "A voice is heard in Ramah, mourning and great weeping, Rachel weeping for her children and refusing to be comforted, because her children are no more" (Jer. 31:15; Matt. 2:18).

Herod's paranoia, then, was fatal—ending in one of the worst episodes in all biblical history. It is so sad to think that the birth of Jesus would be paralleled by such a tragedy. But it did. And yet the Magi, as well as Joseph and Mary, were sovereignly and providentially led in a manner that kept the baby

Jesus safe (Matt. 2:12–13, 19–23). Despite false professions and tragedies that parallel a true move of the Spirit, God's purpose will not be thwarted (Job 42:2), and His elect will be preserved (Matt. 24:24).

John the Baptist

> In those days John the Baptist came, preaching in the Desert of Judea.... People went out to him from Jerusalem and all Judea and the whole region of the Jordan.
>
> —Matthew 3:1, 5

I doubt anybody has come along who has raised the ire and envy of sophisticated religious people as John the Baptist did with the Pharisees and Sadducees. If anybody would make a Pharisee or Sadducee say yuck (or its first-century equivalent), it would have been John the Baptist. His clothes were different, his diet was different, his methods were different, and his message was different. "Confessing their sins, they were baptized by him in the Jordan River" (Matt. 3:6). "Jews of Jerusalem sent priests and Levites to ask him who he was" (John 1:19). "Some Pharisees who had been sent questioned him" (vv. 24–25). John the Baptist stirred up jealousy in the religious authorities as had not been done in years.

Who "sent" them to see John the Baptist? The religious authorities. John the Baptist threatened institutional religion to its very core. The establishment was in serious trouble with a preacher like that at large. What is more, to hear John the

Baptist you had to go a long way—some twenty miles—on foot. Today you can drive from Jerusalem to the Jordan in roughly twenty minutes; in those days it was a good day's journey. When there is an authentic work of God around, people will make any effort to see it, and the enemies of it will make an equal effort to fight it.

Jealousy. "O, beware, my lord of jealousy!" as Shakespeare put it, for "it is the green-eyed monster which doth mock the meat it feeds on." Or as John Milton put it, jealousy is "the injured lover's hell."

Jealous of Jesus?

In a short period of time Jesus became immensely popular (Matt. 4:23–25). This caused some people to say to John the Baptist, assuming he would be jealous of Jesus, "That man who was with you on the other side of the Jordan—the one you testified about—well, he is baptizing, and everyone is going to him" (John 3:26).

Question: Did Jesus's sudden popularity make John the Baptist jealous? Is it really possible that John was just a little bit jealous of Jesus becoming more popular? Yes. I think that is very possible. But John replied with an answer that turns out to be one of the very best ways for you and me to deal with jealousy; it provides us with a rationale of how all of us can overcome envy and jealousy. John replied, "A man can receive only what is given him from heaven" (v. 27). In other words, John the Baptist—even if he was tempted to be jealous—gave the rationale of how to overcome jealousy with that succinct statement about one's anointing or calling. We must accept the extent and limits of our anointing. Not anybody can do everything. We all have a measure of faith. (See Romans 12:3.)

In a word, John knew his place—who he was and what he was called to do. He also knew who Jesus was and what He was called to do: "The Lamb of God, who takes away the sin of the world!" (John 1:29). "He must become greater; I must become less" (John 3:30). That is not only the way John the Baptist felt about Jesus, but it is also the way you and I must regard the next move of the Holy Spirit. The greatest enemy to a current work of the Spirit often comes from those who were at the forefront of the previous work of God. John the Baptist presents us with a perfect model of how to respond when our time has come and gone.

Herod Antipas

When the next Herod—Herod Antipas, also known as "the Tetrarch"—heard that Jesus was performing miracles, he concluded that Jesus was actually John the Baptist raised from the dead! John the Baptist told Herod that it was not lawful for him to have his brother's wife. When the daughter of Herodias was asked by Herod, "Ask me for anything you want, and I'll give it to you," she asked for the head of John the Baptist on a platter. The king was distressed, but because he gave an oath in front of guests, he did not want to refuse her. He had John beheaded (Mark 6:14–29).

Jesus called this Herod a "fox." It was the only time Jesus

gave a nickname to anybody. When told that Herod wanted to kill him, Jesus responded: "Go tell that fox, 'I will drive out demons and heal people today and tomorrow, and on the third day I will reach my goal'" (Luke 13:32).

Later on Jesus stood before Pontius Pilate. Pilate sent Jesus to the same Herod Antipas who had John the Baptist beheaded. "When Herod saw Jesus, he was greatly pleased, because for a long time he had been wanting to see him....He hoped to see him perform some miracle" (Luke 23:8). But when he piled Jesus with questions, Jesus gave him no answer.

That to me was one of Jesus's most brilliant moments. It is the way to confront a jealous person. You say *nothing*. You are in a no-win situation, so don't waste your words! That was the day that Herod and Pilate became friends (Luke 23:12). Herod sent Jesus back to Pilate, and Pilate knew "it was out of *envy* that they had handed Jesus over to him" (Matt. 27:18, emphasis added). If nobody else knew that envy and jealousy were at the bottom of the conspiracy to have Jesus crucified, never forget that Pontius Pilate knew the motive!

KING HEROD AGRIPPA I

The King Herod (the Great) who had baby boys killed around Bethlehem was succeeded some thirty years later by another Herod—Agrippa I. This Herod was of the same ilk. He ordered that James, the brother of John, be put to death. When he saw that this pleased the Jews, he proceeded to seize Peter too (Acts 12:1–3). But Peter was miraculously preserved, not unlike the way in which Jesus, His parents, and the Magi were preserved. It was supernatural (vv. 6–17).

But that is not the end of the story. Later on, on a certain day when Herod, wearing his royal robes, sat on his throne delivering a public address, and the people shouted, "This is the voice of a god, not of a man," God Himself stepped in. Because Herod "did not give praise to God," an angel of the Lord struck him down, "and he was eaten by worms and died" (Acts 12:21–23).

King Herod Agrippa II

Jesus Himself prophesied that the apostle Paul would testify before kings (Acts 9:15). Paul was later on trial and witnessed for Jesus Christ before the last of the Herods mentioned in Scripture. Agrippa II could easily see that Paul was trying to convert him on the spot! "Do you think that in such a short time you can persuade me to be a Christian?" the king asked Paul. Paul indeed tried—but failed, although he was regarded as a lawful person by the king (Acts 26:28–32). A prophecy that one will stand before a king does not mean that king will be converted.

When the great awakening for which we pray finally comes— as I believe it will—you can anticipate some of the things we have seen in this chapter. The common people will receive the gospel. Some powerful people may even be saved. Some, however, not many. Not many that are saved are wise by human standards, "not many were influential; not many were of noble birth. But God chose the foolish things of the world to shame the wise; God chose the weak things of the world to shame the strong...to nullify the things that are, so that no one may boast before him" (1 Cor. 1:26–29).

God is jealous for the gospel. It is designed in such a manner that no person can get glory who embraces it. And those who have the privilege of spreading it must never forget they are unworthy vessels. Never forget the Herod who was eaten of worms because he did not give glory to God. The jealousy of God is nothing to play around with. Once you begin to take glory for yourself, you are in a dangerous state. Don't do it. Be very, very careful to give God all the glory.

Part IV

OVERCOMING JEALOUSY

Chapter Eleven

ACCEPTING OUR CALLING

In a hierarchy every employee tends to rise to his
level of incompetence.... Work is achieved by those
employees who have not yet reached their level of
incompetence.

—LAURENCE J. PETER

Do not think of yourself more highly than you
ought, but rather think of yourself with sober
judgment, in accordance with the measure of faith
God has given you.

—ROMANS 12:3

THE QUESTION IS: how do we *cope* with jealousy—theirs
and ours? And how do we *overcome* the jealousy that
has set in on us?

You will recall that in the introduction I made a distinction
between envy and jealousy, although we must not push the
distinction too far. The main point is this: Envy is inevitable;
jealousy is envy that is *manifested*. Envy is the thought; jealousy

is the obsession. The rule of thumb: deal with envy while it is only in your *thoughts*. That is the best way forward.

But what if undoubted jealousy has now set in, and you feel defeated and helpless? Is it too late? No. Otherwise there is no hope for any of us, and I would not write this book!

I want this chapter to be a clear way forward, whether you are feeling envious—or truly jealous. In whichever state you find yourself, this chapter is for you.

The question then is this: what do you do when you find yourself not only tempted with envy but also bedeviled with jealousy? I answer: begin by *accepting your calling*. Not someone else's calling. Your own calling. Come to terms with what God Himself has called *you* to do. Never forget that when Jesus told Peter how he would die, Peter could only think about John and what would be required of John. Jesus lovingly rebuked Peter: "What is that to you?" (John 21:18–22).

Accepting our calling is a high but humbling privilege and responsibility. Truly accepting your own calling—and not looking over your shoulder—will also keep you out of a lot of trouble! It means that we humbly affirm, but with no blushing, what we are good at; we must equally admit, with perhaps some embarrassment, to what we are not very good at. We therefore must accept the potential and limits of our gifting. The thesis of *The Peter Principle* (written by Dr. Laurence J. Peter) is that people are promoted to the level of their incompetence. A person was doing very well at a lower-paying, less-prestigious job. But owing to ambition or a vacancy, a person is promoted—and gets more pay but is not able to function with ease. They operate at the level of their incompetence, the result being high blood pressure, falling out with everyone around them, marriage breakdown, and burnout. For example, a popular, efficient office manager is doing well. No sweat. No fear. No problems. One day he or she is made general director of the company. In a few months the same person becomes unpopular, can't get the work done, and develops health issues. Was the promotion worth it? No.

But that's in the world. A thesis of my book *The Anointing: Yesterday, Today, Tomorrow* is that the Holy Spirit never promotes us to the level of our incompetence. We may promote ourselves, others may promote us, but not the Holy Spirit. He knows what we are good at, what we are not good at, and what the Father has called us to do.

The way we guarantee we will not be promoted to the level of our incompetence is that we truly look at ourselves *soberly*—with ruthless honesty, knowing that we all have only a "measure" of faith. This means that each of us has a limited measure of the Holy Spirit. You do not have all of God there is. Don't let anybody tell you that you do. Only Jesus had all of God there is (Col. 1:19); only He was given the Holy Spirit without any limit (John 3:34). It is our responsibility, then, to admit humbly to our limitations.

Nobody can do everything. Quit trying to do everything! Do not imitate another's ability. My own anointing functions only when I don't move outside of it but stay in it. When I am under the anointing, I teach, preach, and write with ease and without struggling. When I am under the anointing I write without trying to be pretentious; I teach without trying to impress the scholar in the audience; I preach without trying to be Martyn Lloyd-Jones. But when I write in order to impress a book reviewer, teach to show the scholar how much I know, or preach to sound great, I forfeit the anointing of the Spirit—then and there. Therefore when I begin to struggle I should recognize that God has graciously put an amber light before me to *stop at once*—and realize I am venturing outside my anointing. When I go outside my anointing it is because I did not heed the amber light. When I feel envy it is a caution—there and then—not to try to mimic another's gifting, personality, or calling.

How Do You Find Your Own Calling?

We will need to define some terms. Anointing, gifting, and calling are sometimes used synonymously. Calling refers to vocation: what God has called you to do in life as a career, job, duty, or mission. Anointing is the power of the Spirit on your gifting; it is what makes it flourish. In order to understand what your particular anointing is, you ask yourself: what am I naturally good at? Your gifts are God's hint toward what you should do with your life.

This becomes your calling. You may feel called to a particular profession, to the ministry, to be an artist, singer, or musician. But are you good and at home in this area? Can you preach so well that people *invite* you to preach? Can you draw a picture or paint a scene that causes everybody to say, "Wow!" If you say you are called to be a singer, I ask: can you sing? You certainly are not going to have a career in singing if people do not enjoy hearing you sing. The Baptist preacher Charles Spurgeon used to say that if God calls you to preach, He will give you a pair of lungs.

One day a man who felt called to a career in music ministry sang a song he had written. "The Lord gave this to me," he had said. Having heard him sing it, I should have had the courage to say to him, "The Lord gave it to you because He didn't want it," but I didn't. The truth is, the poem was less than mediocre, the tune far from being catchy, and the poor man couldn't carry a tune in a bucket. I have also had countless people tell me they felt called to preach. I would ask two questions: Are you prepared to go to Bible college or seminary? Do you get invitations to preach? A preaching gift will be generally recognized by people. If you aren't asked to preach, it may be because God has not called you.

We must be true to ourselves in this matter. To quote Shakespeare: "To thine own self be true." It means rugged honesty about yourself.

We may be envious or jealous of another's anointing or calling, but if each of us comes to terms with what God has called *us* to do and accept it without murmuring, we may lessen the likelihood of jealousy. King Saul became jealous of David's anointing (1 Sam. 18:12). And yet, sadly, we all tend to have problems with what God has called *others* to do. I repeat:

Jesus said that it was none of Peter's business how *John* would die; He replied to Peter, "What is that to you? You must follow *me*" (John 21:21–22, emphasis added). So it is with all of us. We may ask, "What about him? What about her? What are You asking them to do?" And God says to each of us: "None of your business—you follow *Me*."

Not only that, but what God has called each of us to do is equally God-glorifying, holy, and sacred, whether that calling refers to the preaching ministry or practice of medicine, being a missionary or a lawyer, whether being a teacher, bus driver, musician, secretary, dentist, bank teller, businessman, waitress, veterinarian, receptionist, maid, astronaut, chef, or computer analyst. My being a minister, then, is no more godly, honorable, or sacred than another person being a "layman" (if I may use that term). What God calls each of us to do is a holy matter. The issue is whether we obey His calling and come to terms with our own anointing.

We are dealing with two things, then: (1) one's calling, and (2) the ability—anointing—to fulfill that calling. To discover what your calling is, you ask hard questions: What are you good at? What comes easily? What do people say you are good at? What you are good at is God's hint as to what you should do in your life. Caution: Don't look over your shoulder and envy what another can do better than you. Don't wish you were called to do what they are called to do. After all, the calling comes from God.

One of the most important verses to help with envy and

jealousy is in Paul's provocative question: "For who makes you different from anyone else? What do you have that you did not receive? And if you did receive it, why do you boast as though you did not?" (1 Cor. 4:7). Who takes the responsibility for our calling? The buck stops with God.

Sometimes people have ambition not only to do what they are unable to do but also to do things they don't really enjoy. Some only fear they won't be admired if they don't excel or climb up the prestige ladder. But if *God* isn't keen on my excelling or climbing up the glory ladder, do I still want to make that climb? When I keep in mind that God wants not only what is in *His* interest but also what is best for *me*, why should I worry when I accept that sober truth that I am no Charles Spurgeon, Albert Einstein, or Winston Churchill? Why would I want the limelight when I am not competent to function in that arena? Or why should I be jealous that I don't get invited to see the prime minister or president—when others have (in God's strategic purpose) earned the right to be there? He could have made me fit in that regard—but chose not to! My response: Yes, Lord. Your sovereign will be done. Amen.

It is not a very prudent man or woman who is jealous for power and prestige but doesn't have the ability to perform very well should they get what they want. This is the point of the book *The Peter Principle*. People often get what they want but can't do the job! Dr. Peter reckons that the reason a country, university, hospital, church, school, department store, society, business, or government functions so pitifully is because everybody from the top down has been promoted to the level of their incompetence. Ambition leads people to do crazy things, and all of us pay dearly. Whether it be heads of state, church leaders, or department store managers, there are those who should not be in these positions of responsibility.

What put these people in these positions? Often the answer is jealousy. They were motivated by a dogged determination to show everyone what they could do. They were jealous of the ones who previously had the high-paying, prestigious jobs; they wanted to move in so the same people would now be jealous of them!

I therefore say that one of the best ways to cure jealousy is to accept your calling from God—humbly. Do not aspire to be where—if you got what you wanted—you might be totally miserable. Do not covet a job He does not have in mind for you. The Lord will not promote you to the level of your incompetence; why should *you* do it?

One more thing: He is able to promote you to the job you want—if it is the precise one you are supposed to have. You say, "I am more qualified than the person who has that job—or who is applying for that job." I reply: if you are the Lord's, no good thing will He withhold from you (Ps. 84:11). You may be *more* qualified than anybody—and see a less able person occupying the job you want; but if He has chosen to give the job to another person, is not that His prerogative? What if your time has not come? What if succeeding would be worse for you because you are not ready for success? George Bernard Shaw once said,

"There are two tragedies in life: one is not to get the desire of your heart; the other is to get it."

It is sometimes pseudo guilt (false guilt that God did not put there) that motivates a person to get to the top. They feel they are somehow letting themselves down (or perhaps their parents) if they don't succeed in their ambition. But when we realize that it is *God* who does the promoting, why would anybody want to upstage God's own choice of whom He wants to exalt? "No one from the east or the west or from the desert can exalt a man. But it is God who judges: he brings one down, he exalts another" (Ps. 75:6–7).

This brings us back to a verse I raised in my introduction: "How can you believe if you accept praise from one another, yet make no effort to obtain the praise that comes from the only God?" (John 5:44). I cannot begin to tell you how much this verse has comforted me over the years. I have sought to live by this principle more than any other. It has helped defuse my anger, dilute my ambition, take the pressure off to get ahead, decrease my envy, and militate against jealousy. Why? What *God* thinks I should do is all that matters. Why should I be jealous when it is *He* who has exalted another to a position and chooses to keep me where I am? The buck stops with God. Otherwise it is God I am angry with and jealous of—and I don't want to be found doing that.

"He chose our inheritance for us," said the psalmist (Ps. 47:4). This means He decided in advance where He wanted us to be in a given time. First of all, He chose the time and place of our birth—the place, parents, and circumstances (Acts 17:26). We had no control over our birth. We did not choose our parents; God did. We did not choose the time and place of our birth; God did.

Secondly, He gave us our bodies—even while we were in our mother's womb. "I am fearfully and wonderfully made; your works are wonderful, I know that full well. My frame was not hidden from you when I was made in the secret place. When I was woven together in the depths of the earth, your eyes saw my unformed body" (Ps. 139:14–16). This means our brains were formed by Him. Our intelligence was determined by Him. We no doubt can improve on how well and clearly we think, but our basic ability is already set—like it or not. Wow. I love this. It takes the pressure off to perform! Why be jealous of the person who is cleverer than I when it is God who gave them their superior brain?

Third, "A man can receive only what is given him from heaven" (John 3:27). Those were John the Baptist's words. It was his reply to the observation that Jesus was gaining more disciples, getting bigger crowds, and upstaging John's popularity. How did John cope? His answer was that *God in heaven* is the one who bestows success, blessing, favor, and grace. It was easy, therefore, for John to say, "He must become greater; I must become less" (v. 30). Was John tempted to jealousy? Almost certainly. And this is how he coped.

So with our calling. The same God who gives and withholds mercy is the one who determines our calling. And talent. And promotion. He opens and closes doors. Either way it is in our interest. Be thankful for the closed door as much as you rejoice in the open door. He calls some to be doctors, some to be nurses, some to be preachers, some to be computer experts, some to be astronauts, some to be secretaries, some to be scientists, some to be lawyers, some to be firemen, some to be policemen, some to be politicians, some to be executives, and some to have *little or no profile whatsoever.*

To the non-Christian and the one not devoted to God's glory, this chapter will not only make no sense, but it could also be dismissed out of hand. But to the person who aspires to please God, I predict that a great victory over envy and jealousy will come to the present reader of this book. God wants you to have peace, not anger; He wants you to be full of love, not jealousy. The way forward is to accept your calling from God, not what He has chosen for someone else. When I discover when He opens the door for someone else—and not for me—I *may* be a little bit disappointed, yes, but I am nonetheless pacified when I know that "no good thing does he withhold from those whose walk is blameless" (Ps. 84:11).

I have lived long enough to value the closed door as much as the open door. Not only that, but I have also watched Him work best when I do not raise a little finger to make things happen. To be honest, I am scared to death of trying to make something happen: I may get what I want—and be *so sorry.*

Through making ten thousand mistakes and waiting on God over my seventy-odd years, I have learned to accept not only my calling but also my imperfections, limited ability, disappointments, enemies' unflattering comments, enemies' promotions, rejections, relationships turned sour, and friends getting ahead. I have also learned to cope with enigmas and unanswered prayers.

God chose our inheritance, He chose our calling, and He bestows the anointing. The buck stops with Him. The way to deal with our jealousy is to let God be God and accept what He gives—and what He doesn't give.

Chapter Twelve

KEEPING JEALOUSY AT BAY

If you go to the left, I'll go to the right; if you go to the right, I'll go to the left.

—Genesis 13:9

I would be speaking the truth. But I refrain, so no one will think more of me than is warranted by what I do or say.

—2 Corinthians 12:6

Blood's thicker than water.

—Scottish Proverb

I T IS LIKELY that you will overcome jealousy in proportion to the way you keep both your friends and enemies from being jealous of you. As long as you are wanting them to be jealous of you, you reveal you are still jealous of them. But if you reach the place that it pains you for them to be jealous of you, it is a good thing.

Like it or not, people will be jealous of you. "I have nothing that would make them jealous," you may say. But they will still be jealous of you. They will find something. There is that in you that makes another person envy. You may not think it, but it is true. You may have a low opinion of yourself, but there will be something about you—whether your appearance, personality, gifting, job, friends, background, or opportunities—which will make them envious. You simply cannot make everybody like you.

It is our responsibility, when possible, to avoid the onslaught of jealousy from others. We should never want to make people feel jealous. We should practice the Golden Rule ("Do to others as you would have them do to you"—Luke 6:31), always being sensitive to their feelings and fragile egos. It is wicked when we knowingly make another person feel jealous—or to set them up to feel jealous. We should learn how to see it coming—both in ourselves and in others. We should carefully avoid comments or situations that we know are likely to make people jealous. In much the same way that we should make no provision for the flesh to fulfill the lust thereof (since the best way to avoid falling into sin is to avoid the temptation that could make us vulnerable—Romans 13:14), so too we should learn what will make other people jealous—and never go there.

And yet making a person feel jealous is sometimes an easy thing to do, and sometimes it seems so innocent. How often have we sent postcards to our friends from an exotic place in order to say, "Wish you were here"—a probable euphemism for saying, "Hope this makes you feel a bit jealous!" So often the true motivation for being seen with the right people, getting the coveted invitation, or acquiring a new car or set of clothes is to see others envy us a bit. Jesus would never intentionally make a person feel jealous.

Jealousy often gives birth to the most heinous words and deeds. Can you imagine Jesus purposefully making people jealous? No! He never—ever—did anything that was designed to make people feel jealous.

Jealousy can precipitate a major crisis. The best way to deal with a crisis is to anticipate it and avoid it. Likewise the best way to cope with jealousy is to anticipate it and avoid it. Once its seed is planted and then grows, it is hard to manage. If you can sense the seed of jealousy about to be planted, step in at once and stop it. If, however, it gets planted, make every effort to pluck it out at the roots as soon as possible.

JEALOUSY IN THE EARLY CHURCH

The first crisis the Christian church encountered came through persecution—largely from the Sadducees who objected to the teaching of the resurrection of Jesus from the dead. But the first major crisis in the earliest church from *within* started from the potential jealous feelings that were beginning to surface among Greek Jews toward Hebrew-speaking Jews. The well-known Scottish proverb says, "Blood's thicker than water," which means that our family relationships triumph over other friendships at the end of the day. This, of course, is not always true, but racial rivalry and national rivalry—which we examined in chapter 3—will often surface in the most unlikely places.

There were basically two categories of Jews in ancient times: Hebraic Jews and Greek Jews. Both were of the same blood, yes. But Hebrew Jews somehow managed to feel they were a cut above Grecian Jews. You often have this where a particular language is spoken. Take Spanish. The people of Spain often feel they are superior to Mexicans, Cubans, and Puerto Ricans— although Spanish is spoken by all these. There is something about the "mother country" that gives it a feeling of superi- ority—causing rivalry and jealousy. You have it in the English language. English is spoken around the world. The mother country's English is the most attractive (if only I had a British accent) and the English people tend to feel superior to all other countries—including Wales, Ireland, and Scotland!

You had this when it came to Hebrew Jews. They felt they had antiquity on their side in a way that Greek Jews did not. This was not fair, of course, but those Jews in ancient Israel that spoke *only* Hebrew felt they had a prestige and clout that did not belong to Greek Jews. For one thing, the Grecian Jews read only the Septuagint, the Greek translation of the Old Testa- ment. Hebrew Jews could boast that they read the original Hebrew Old Testament. Moreover, they spoke the language of Abraham, Isaac, Jacob, David, and all the prophets.

But Christian converts in the earliest church came from both Hebrew Jews and Greek Jews. "In those days when the number of disciples was increasing, the Grecian Jews among them complained against the Hebraic Jews because their widows were being overlooked in the daily distribution of food" (Acts

6:1). The Greek-speaking Jews felt they were being marginalized and passed by—all because of their ethnic origin. Not only did this squabble need to be defused, but it was also sapping the strength of the leadership; the apostles were being diverted from preaching the gospel and having to attend to petty rivalries, even though they were serious.

God gave them a brilliant solution: deacons. This is when deacons first came into the church. "It would not be right for us to neglect the ministry of the word of God in order to wait on tables" (Acts 6:2). So they chose seven men full of the Holy Spirit and wisdom. Seven deacons were chosen and ordained. The result: "The word of God spread. The number of disciples in Jerusalem increased rapidly, and a large number of priests became obedient to the faith" (Acts 6:7).

You can be sure that Satan was behind the quarreling. You can be sure that things might have gotten out of hand and the crisis made far, far worse, but the apostles acted wisely and kept jealousy at bay—and God put His seal on the whole matter.

ABRAHAM AND LOT: TERRITORIAL JEALOUSY

That is what Abraham did. He kept jealousy at bay. Whether it was his shrewdness or an absence of greed, I only know that Abraham managed to avoid a huge blowup with his relative Lot when the issue of who occupies which territory emerged. This incident may have been the first biblical account of territorial jealousy; it has been going on ever since, especially in that part of the world.

Both Abraham and Lot had become prosperous, so much so that "the land could not support them while they stayed together" (Gen. 13:6). The result was that quarreling arose between the herdsmen of Abraham and Lot. Abraham stepped in and said to Lot, "Let's not have any quarreling between you and me, or between your herdsmen and mine, for we are brothers. Is not the whole land before you? Let's part company. If you go to the left, I'll go to the right; if you go to the right, I'll go to the left" (vv. 8–9).

Abraham might have put it differently. He knew perfectly well that the whole plain of the Jordan was "well watered, like the garden of the LORD" (v. 10), and Abraham therefore could have insisted on having it for himself. But this would have caused jealousy and a further quarrel with Lot. Abraham was more eager to keep Lot from jealous feelings and avoid the messy spectacle of a family squabble than he was to have the better part of the land. Abraham therefore took the high road: he let Lot choose. He no doubt knew what Lot would choose. Surprise, surprise, Lot chose the plain of the Jordan that was well watered—"the whole plain of the Jordan and set out toward the east" and then "pitched his tents near Sodom" (vv. 11–12). It turned out to be a bad move for Lot, not because of the fertility of the land but because of its proximity to Sodom. "The men of Sodom were wicked and were sinning greatly against the LORD" (v. 13). Perhaps Lot saw all the greenery and fancied that the people there are so well off and happy. The grass often looks greener on the other side of the fence, but it seldom is.

The phrase "pitched his tent toward Sodom" (Gen. 13:12, KJV) is one of the most ominous phrases in Holy Writ. Whatever translation, these words should be understood as a warning to all of us not to see how close we can get to the world but how far removed we can be. Some think it is a sign of strength to see how close you can get to temptation—then resist it. Wrong. True strength is refusing to go where you know temptation is likely to show up.

Why did Abraham let Lot choose? It was as though Abraham was willing to flip a coin to decide. He honestly did not care! Was it shrewdness or detachment from material things that led him to let Lot decide? It was both, but I would argue that the shrewdness came from Abraham's lack of greed. The lack of greed sprang from the promise God had given to Abraham. That promise gave Abraham something to live for. His eyes were now focused on something greater than anybody else had envisaged. God had said to him, "I will make you into a great nation and I will bless you; I will make your name great, and you will be a blessing. I will bless those who bless you, and whoever curses you I will curse; and all peoples on earth will be blessed through you" (Gen. 12:2–3). A promise like that gives one something to live for! It makes the things of this world to grow strangely dim.

Abraham was commanded by God to leave his country, his people, and his father's household to seek for a land he knew nothing about. Abraham obeyed "even though he did not know where he was going" (Heb. 11:8). It was a good move. He would not have made the move had he not truly believed God's promise. Abraham's obedience resulted in wisdom. Obedience to God always does result in true wisdom. "The fear of the LORD is the beginning of wisdom, and knowledge of the Holy One is understanding" (Prov. 9:10).

Abraham had something going for him that Lot apparently did not have. Therefore it was a small thing for Abraham to say to Lot, "If you go to the left, I'll go to the right; if you go to the right, I'll go to the left" (Gen. 13:9).

One of the best ways to keep jealousy at bay is having something to live for that is infinitely greater than the things of this world. Paul told us to set our hearts on "things above, where Christ is seated at the right hand of God. Set your minds on things above, not on earthly things" (Col. 3:1–2). By not being covetous for the better part of the land Abraham avoided dwelling near Sodom—a blessing far greater than he could have known.

Wisdom has as a fringe benefit of far more blessings than we realize at first. In fact, wisdom almost always begins with no proof one has gotten it right. You make the right choice; you feel nothing. You make the fear of the Lord a priority; you wonder if you were right. Like the psalmist, at first you envy the arrogant when you see the prosperity of the wicked and hastily conclude: "Surely in vain have I kept my heart pure; in vain have I washed my hands in innocence" (Ps. 73:13). Until, he continued, "I entered the sanctuary of God; then I understood their final destiny. Surely you placed them on slippery ground; you cast them down to ruin" (vv. 17–18).

Yes, you may have to wait awhile to receive all the benefits of wisdom. But they are worth waiting for, not to mention things in between that you are saved from. "Wisdom will save you from the ways of wicked men, from men whose words are perverse.... It will save you also from the adulteress, from the wayward wife with her seductive words" (Prov. 2:12, 16). Abraham could not have known that his inner detachment from the entire matter was simultaneously sparing him the agony that bedeviled Lot later on. All because he avoided a family fight, one that almost certainly would have been over getting the upper hand on Lot regarding territory.

"For the love of money is a root of all kinds of evil. Some people, eager for money, have wandered from the faith and pierced themselves with many griefs" (1 Tim. 6:10). The person who escapes the love of money (a remarkable accomplishment) will be the least likely to succumb to jealousy regarding earthly things. Abraham had so much to live for that it was a small thing for him to say to Lot, "If you go to the left, I'll go to the right; if you go to the right, I'll go to the left" (Gen. 13:9).

What, then, might grip us so that we can, like Abraham, keep jealousy at bay? I answer: living by the promises of God. He has given us "very great and precious promises, so that through them you may participate in the divine nature and escape the corruption in the world caused by evil desires" (2 Pet. 1:4). When we are *gripped* by the gospel, the promise of heaven, the promise that God will supply all our needs, the promise that no good thing will He withhold from them who walk uprightly, and the promise that He has a carefully thought-out plan for each of our lives, we will be in a good place indeed. Jealousy will have a much harder time getting its grip on us when we have something better to live for. And we are not ready to live until we are ready to die. And when we are ready to die, knowing—as Abraham did—that we are eventually going to heaven, we are ready to live!

I don't mean to be unfair, but I have often feared that the "prosperity gospel" (sometimes called "health and wealth gospel") plays immediately and directly into people's greed more than it does their fear of God. It is no sign of spirituality to get excited over the idea of God existing for our earthly happiness. When I listen to some preachers, however well meaning they may be, it seems to me they are appealing to the unregenerate part of man's nature rather than our life in Christ when they focus on our fleshly interests rather than God's interests.

Abraham was wealthy not because that was his goal but because God chose to bless him. Abraham's heartbeat and focus was living by the promises of God. And when God said to him one day, "Look up at the heavens and count the stars—if indeed you can count them," Abraham believed it! This is amazing when you think about it. Already up in years with an aging barren wife, Abraham still believed God. As a consequence of believing this very unlikely promise, God "credited" Abraham with righteousness (Gen. 15:6), this being Paul's chief example for his teaching of justification by faith alone (Rom. 4).

Abraham accomplished more than anybody in his day. Indeed, he accomplished more than anybody described in the Book of Genesis. He got more space in Hebrews 11 (the faith chapter of the Bible) than all the other famous people of faith. Why? "He was looking forward to the city with foundations, whose architect and builder is God" (Heb. 11:10). Abraham was on his way to heaven! That is what he had his sights on! This is why it was a simple matter for Abraham to let Lot decide where they were going to live here below. The truth is, those who are the most enamored with the hope of eternal life and focused on heaven will achieve more on earth than those whose only hope is in this life.

After Lot and Abraham parted, the Lord said to Abraham, "All the land that you see I will give to you and your offspring forever" (Gen. 13:15). Not only that; Lot found himself in difficulty when he got caught later in the crossfire in a war between the kings. Abraham rescued Lot and was blessed with more material goods than ever. It is when Melchizedek king of Salem appeared to bless Abraham and Abraham became the first tither. Abraham gave Melchizedek "a tenth of everything" (Gen. 14:20). By Abraham's absence of greed and keeping jealousy at bay, God blessed him more than ever. When you realize that this life is not all there is, you are more likely to enjoy it more; by focusing on it, you forfeit it. "For whoever wants to save his life will lose it, but whoever loses his life for me and the gospel will save it," said Jesus (Mark 8:35).

Further evidence of Abraham's detachment from greed was his refusal to accept any of the booty from the king of Sodom. Abraham even took an oath in which he vowed to "accept nothing" from the king of Sodom, lest it be said he made Abraham rich (Gen. 14:22–23). This is remarkable and set a historical precedent for a believer. Some might say, "All money belongs to God," and therefore would have no qualms over receiving what comes from a wicked king. But not Abraham. He took the view there is such a thing as poisonous money. Money isn't everything. The apostle Paul went even further, rebuking the Corinthians for Christians suing one another. "Why not rather be wronged? Why not rather be cheated?" (1 Cor. 6:7). How many of us are willing to be cheated or wronged in order to uphold the integrity of the gospel and testimony of the church?

Dr. O. S. Hawkins put it like this: "The principle hindrance to the advancement of the kingdom of God is greed. It is the chief obstacle to heaven-sent revival. It seems that when the back of greed is broken, the human spirit soars into the region of unselfishness." O. S. said this in the context of giving and calls for "hilarious giving," which he believes will bring revival. But detachment from material things is much the same thing. It could well be that when we are like Abraham not only with regard to faith in the promises of God but also giving to Him and detachment from material things, the revival we long and pray for will be at hand.

This life is not all there is. Our present existence is temporary. We are all living in tents—our mortal bodies. "We know that if the earthly tent we live in is destroyed, we have a building from God, an eternal house in heaven, not built by human hands" (2 Cor. 5:1). I fear, however, there are too many of us who plan for life here below as though there were no heaven! We are too much like the man in one of Jesus's parables who produced a good crop. He thought to himself, "'I will tear down my barns and build bigger ones, and there I will store all my grain and my goods. And I'll say to myself, "You have plenty of good things laid up for many years. Take life easy; eat, drink and be merry."' But God said to him, 'You fool! This very night your life will be demanded from you. Then who will get what you have prepared for yourself?'" Jesus concluded this parable by saying, "This is how it will be with anyone who stores up things for himself but is not rich toward God" (Luke 12:18–21).

One of the great fringe benefits of focusing on God's promises to us, then, is God granting us the wisdom that anticipates and avoids jealousy. Abraham was not a jealous man.

I've always admired Deborah the prophetess for being sensitive to Barak's male ego. She told him what to do to defeat the enemy. He replied, "If you go with me, I will go; but if you don't go with me, I won't go." She went along with him but cautioned: "Because of the way you are going about this, the honor will not be yours, for the LORD will hand Sisera over to a woman" (Judges 4:8–9). Deborah was trying to keep jealousy at bay.

There are people who literally live to make people jealous. This is what excites them. It is what motivates them. It is all they have to live for. Their jewelry. Their silverware and china. Their home. Their location. Their cars. Their possessions. Whom they know. Their pedigree. Take away the thought of people's envy, and these things mean nothing to them. Like the Pharisees and their pious acts—"All they do is done for men to see" (Matt. 23:5). So it is with greedy people; they live to be envied.

Jealousy is painful. I know what it is to be hurt because I was overlooked when others were noticed. I remember someone deliberately phoning me from a party they were invited to—knowing I too wanted to be there but wasn't invited—to make me feel envious. It worked. It ruined my day, but it shouldn't have. When earthly things are too important to us, we are exceedingly vulnerable to the pain of jealousy. But when we have worthwhile things to live for and heaven to look forward to, we minimize the way the devil can bring us down through jealous feelings.

Abraham spared Lot the pain of jealousy by letting him have what he wanted. As it turned out in the end, all was not so good for Lot, but Abraham had no way of knowing that. The truth is, Abraham exemplified the peace and ease that one has in life when greed is held at bay.

Chapter Thirteen

THE JEALOUSY OF GOD

Do not worship any other god, for the LORD, whose
name is Jealous, is a jealous God.

—Exodus 34:14

That didn't feel right in my spirit.[1]

—Oprah Winfrey

I T COULD BE easily argued that the jealousy of God is the
most offensive thing about God. From the standpoint of the
non-Christian, God's jealousy is possibly the most undesir-
able trait about God's character. When God revealed His name
as being *Jealous,* He was certainly not putting His "best foot
forward" to the world. On the other hand, He did not reveal
Himself like this to the world in the first place; He did so to His
covenant people—Israel. In any case, God's jealousy is possibly
the one thing about the God of the Bible that the world dislikes
most about Him.

Jonathan Edwards, probably the greatest theologian in
American history, taught us many things. Among them was the
fact that there is one thing Satan the great counterfeiter cannot

successfully counterfeit—namely, an unfeigned love for the pure glory of God. Loving the honor and glory of God is a way a believer may know for sure that he or she is truly converted. For when we *love the glory of God*, it proves we have truly been given a new nature and a measure of the Holy Spirit that defy a natural explanation. Only *God* can give a person a love for His glory. The flesh cannot duplicate that!

If there is anything that the worldly, secular, and unregenerate person hates, it is the glory of God. The God of glory is "man's natural enemy," says Jonathan Edwards. Therefore when a person falls in love with the glory of God, he or she may be absolutely sure they are the Lord's! The flesh cannot remotely produce that. It is not possible. Only God Himself can produce this. That is why a love for the glory of God is evidence that a person is *saved* and not lost.

The glory of God is the sum total of all His attributes (characteristics). Theologians talk about God's attributes—His omniscience (He knows everything), His omnipresence (He is everywhere), His omnipotence (He is all-powerful), His sovereignty (His right to do what he chooses to do), His justice (He must punish sin), His mercy (He doesn't want to punish us), and His *jealousy* (His zero tolerance of a rival). But the glory of God is the sum total of all these attributes. In other words, the *one word* that encompasses all these attributes is God's *glory*.

The glory of God, however, is closely akin to the jealousy of God. The glory of God refers to His honor, esteem, weightiness, sovereignty, and power. The jealousy of God refers to His intolerance for any rival. He will not brook a rival—not even a little bit and not for a moment. He therefore affirms His Son's word: "*I* am the way and the truth and the life. No one comes to the Father except through *me*" (John 14:6, emphasis added). Jesus mirrors the God of the Bible in these words.

GOD'S NAME IS JEALOUS

We have seen in this book that jealousy is generally not a very attractive characteristic. Jealousy can be ugly, off-putting, disgusting, sickening, and even fatal—leading one to kill. There is very little that is nice about jealousy other than the way God can use it to advance His purposes. So jealousy is not usually good.

But like it or not, Jealous is the very *name* of the God of Scripture. "Do not worship any other god, for the LORD, whose name is Jealous, is a jealous God" (Exod. 34:14). In other words, God does not hide this fact about Himself. He does not try to put a good face forward, saving the worse for last (when you find out what He is really like). No. God is "up front" about His nature. He is a jealous God. No apologies. No explanations. No effort to make us like Him. He does not say, "Wait. Give Me a chance to show you how nice I am." Whoever said that God was nice? He's *good* but not nice.

I've often been amazed that the apostle Paul was like this concerning Jesus. Paul said he calculated, before entering Corinth, that he would make no effort to make Jesus look "good" to worldly people. "I resolved," said Paul, "to know nothing

195

while I was with you except Jesus Christ and him crucified" (1 Cor. 2:2). Paul put Jesus's "worst foot forward," if I may put it that way. When you realize what crucifixion meant to the ancient Hellenistic world, you may have thought nobody would ever want to be converted to Jesus—knowing that He died on a cross. Not the best advertisement for God's Messiah. But Paul knew that no one would be saved for sure until they heard and embraced this very gospel, so he decided to begin and end with this message!

God does this too with Himself. He admits to being the very kind of God that worldly people hate most. So in the Ten Commandments He reveals His jealousy.

It should not surprise us, then, that unregenerate people hate a jealous God and a God of glory. It goes against the grain as much as anything we could imagine. There is nothing about it that would appeal to a natural human being. What it does, furthermore, is expose where one's heart is. If a love for the glory of God is a way of proving that one is truly a Christian, so too a hatred for the glory or jealousy of God is a way of showing that one's heart is not right with God.

WHO IS OPRAH ANYWAY?

Like most Americans, I love Oprah Winfrey. I watched her for years when we lived in England. I am amazed how far she has come. It is said she is now the most powerful woman in the world. She is both lovely and lovable; she is also brilliant, not to mention wealthy, charismatic, and incalculably influential. What a woman like that could do for God!

But Oprah has chosen to reject the God of the Bible. She has been open about this and told us why. I heard her tell how she listened to the preacher in a Baptist church when she was twenty-seven or twenty-eight years old. The preacher was waxing eloquently about the omniscience, omnipresence, and omnipotence of God. So far, so good. Oprah was apparently enthralled—until he quoted Exodus 34:14, that God is a jealous God. "I was…caught up in the rapture of that moment; until he said 'jealous.'" She said it made her realize, "God is all, God is omnipresent, God is—and God's also jealous? God is jealous of me?" She added, "Something about that didn't feel right in my spirit because I believe that God is love…"[2]

I don't want to be unfair to Oprah, but that fact that the jealousy of God did not feel "right" in her "spirit" is not surprising. Does she feel that her spirit is an infallible test of what is right about God? Who is Oprah (or anyone for that matter) to assume that what she *feels* in her spirit is a reliable test concerning ultimate truth? Oprah Winfrey usually does not come through as being arrogant but rather honest and vulnerable. But not this time. Why *should* God's jealousy feel right in her spirit? It shouldn't. Neither was it intended to. God is holy; we are sinners. There is nothing about God's purest nature that we sinful creatures should naturally like. "Do not be quick with your mouth, do not be hasty in your heart to utter anything before God. God is in heaven and you are on earth, so let your words be few" (Eccles. 5:2).

God's Jealousy Proves His Love

True conversion is crossing over a line between darkness and light, between truth and lie, between what is natural-type thinking and what is beyond nature. Only the Holy Spirit can change the way a person thinks about the true God. The Holy Spirit makes Jesus's death on the cross a glorious matter. The same Holy Spirit makes the jealousy of God a sweet revelation to the regenerated spirit.

We should *love* it that God is jealous of us. *This shows how much He loves you and me.* If He didn't love me, He wouldn't even *care* when I cast my eyes toward the world, when I become enamoured with the flesh, and when I listen to His archenemy the devil. God only wants what is best for us. It is His jealousy of us that keeps us from ruining our lives. His jealousy is our insurance policy that we won't harm ourselves and miss what is best in our lives.

The jealousy of God is therefore the proof of His love. If Oprah only realized that what she dislikes about God—what didn't make her feel "right" in her spirit—is what she should adore about Him!

This is why the first commandment reads, "You shall have no other gods before me," followed by the second commandment: "You shall not make for yourself an idol in the form of anything in heaven above or on the earth beneath or in the waters below.

You shall not bow down to them or worship them; for I, the Lord your God, am a jealous God, punishing the children for the sin of the fathers to the third and fourth generation of those who hate me, but showing love to a thousand generations of those who love me and keep my commandments" (Exod. 20:3–6).

By the way, it really is *true*. The jealousy of God is a no-joke, no-nonsense matter. He really *is* jealous. He will show it. He is no respecter of persons. He won't bend this principle for any of us. This is the God who is revealed throughout Scripture—in the Old Testament and the New Testament—as one who will show up because He is Jealous. He swore in His wrath that the children of Israel would not enter His rest—and they *didn't*, although they tried (Heb. 3:11; Num. 14:40–45). Even Moses could not enter the Promised Land because he disobeyed God's command (Deut. 32:51–52).

We are talking about the very same God with whom we have to do today. He is the same God. "I the Lord do not change" (Mal. 3:6). I'm sorry, but God is everlastingly jealous. However, He is also *merciful*. This means He does not want to punish us. I think my favorite verse in all the Book of Psalms is this: "He knows how we are formed, he remembers that we are dust" (Ps. 103:14). I can hardly read that verse sometimes without coming to tears. A similar verse is this: "He remembered that they were but flesh" (Ps. 78:39). He is jealous, yes. But He is equally gracious. This is why James could say (and, oh, how we should be thankful for this): "Mercy triumphs over judgment!" (James 2:13).

This is why we should humbly ask God—daily—for His mercy. The first thing we should ask for, according to the writer of Hebrews, is *mercy.* "Let us then approach the throne of grace with confidence, *so that we may receive mercy* and find grace to help us in our time of need" (Heb. 4:16, emphasis added). Nobody ever outgrows the need of God's mercy. This is the way we are initially converted (pleading "God, have mercy on me, a sinner"—Luke 18:13), and yet we are in need of mercy as long as we live. Let the most holy and godly person heed these words: we are in daily need of His mercy.

And yet at the same time we must be conscious that God is jealous. He may rebuke us—discipline us—as a sign of His love. Whom the Lord loves He disciplines (Heb. 12:6). It is because God is simultaneously just and merciful, loving and jealous. *That is the way He is.*

The jealousy of God is revealed in Scripture as both positive and negative. Positively, "the LORD will be jealous for his land and take pity on his people" (Joel 2:18). "I am very jealous for Jerusalem and Zion"—which is positive, "but I am very angry with the nations that feel secure," which is negative (Zech. 1:14–15). "God struck down some of the men of Beth Shemesh, putting seventy [some manuscripts say 50,070] of them to death because they had looked into the ark of the LORD" (1 Sam. 6:19). Uzzah was instantly struck dead for putting his hand on the ark of God (2 Sam. 6:7). But it led King David to investigate what had gone wrong; namely, they went against the prescriptions of the Law (1 Chron. 15:13). If we take the care to find out, we will see that there is a reason God manifests His jealousy. It is for our good.

For example, we are temples of the Holy Spirit, that is, our very bodies. "Do you not know that your body is a temple of the Holy Spirit, who is in you, whom you have received from God? You are not your own; you were brought at a price. Therefore honor God with your body" (1 Cor. 6:19–20). Our being temples of the Holy Spirit is directly connected to God's jealousy generally and His jealousy of us in particular. "You are not your own" mirrors God's jealousy; we are His, not ours.

FATHER KNOWS BEST

Most of us realize that some parents want to live their lives through their children. Sometimes a mother will want to live her life through her daughter. There may be many reasons for this, possibly because the mother hopes that her daughter will accomplish what the mother failed to achieve. But sometimes a daughter will resent this, feeling that she should live her own life—and will want her mother to stay out! My own father admitted to living his life through me to some extent. It did not bother me. He always wondered if he should have been a minister of the gospel. He had searched his heart again and again and concluded he was never called of God. However, it would give him some satisfaction if I were called to preach. I was. This way my dad could live his life through me and feel I was in some way a compensation for what he did not achieve.

God wants to live through us. Not to compensate, not to achieve, not because He has ever had a failure, but because He is jealous. He knows what is best for us. He knows what is out there. He Himself is a holy God, and He has zero intolerance for what is evil in our lives. He lives through us by the Holy Spirit. His temple therefore is not in Jerusalem; it is my body. It is your body. It refers mainly to two things: holiness and health. There is often a close connection to holiness and health. All the commands, even those in the Mosaic Law regarding diet, are with regard to holiness (being different from the world) and having healthy bodies. We as Christians are not under the Law (Gal. 5:18), being delivered from its curse. Furthermore, Jesus pronounced all foods "clean" (Mark 7:19). But as Dr. Don Colbert puts it, being delivered from the curse of the Law does not mean we should want to be delivered from the wisdom of it. We should be careful what we bring into our bodies.

However, the word of Paul about our being temples of the Holy Spirit was in the context of sexual purity. "Flee from sexual immorality. All other sins a man commits are outside his body, but he who sins sexually sins against his own body" (1 Cor. 6:18). Sexual purity will go a long way in keeping a man or a woman physically healthy. The whole world knows that diseases that are traced to sexual immorality (for example, AIDS) could be stopped if people would live by the Word of God. But there is that in humankind that resents having to be under any structure. Monogamous heterosexual marriage is the healthiest recipe in the world, but we hate a jealous God—the very concept that would bring us peace and happiness.

THE GOSPEL MESSAGE MIRRORS GOD'S JEALOUSY

The very gospel of Jesus Christ mirrors the jealousy of God in bold relief. First, Jesus presents Himself as the only way to God and the only way to heaven. "I am the way and the truth and the life" (John 14:6). This is arguably the most offensive statement Jesus ever uttered. It certainly does not sit well with the world—now less than ever. The same people who claim to admire Jesus and His teachings still cannot cope with His claim to be the only way. And yet the earliest church echoed this premise to their fingertips: "Salvation is found in no one else, for there is no other name under heaven given to men by which we must be saved" (Acts 4:12).

Secondly, the gospel is so designed that you and I can take no credit or glory—not even a little bit—if we are saved. Reason:

1. God chose us—we did not choose Him, which takes any possibility of individual merit out of our hands in one stroke (Acts 13:48).

2. The Holy Spirit regenerated us, which means that we did not give ourselves life; He gave it through our being born again (John 1:13; 3:3). We did not ask to be born; we did not consult our parents before we

were born, neither did we cause our new birth. God did it all. This is pretty humbling.

3. We are justified not by our personal righteousness but totally and only by the righteousness of Christ, which is put to our credit (Rom. 4:5). In other words, our righteousness is not our own; it is solely and wholly the very obedience of Jesus that is imputed to us. Paul asked, "Where, then, is boasting?" and answered, "It is excluded" (Rom. 3:27).

Bottom line: God will not share His glory; He takes it all.

To be honest, I love this. Do you?

The jealousy of God should therefore have an effect on our lives. As I said, it is a no-joke thing. Its effect upon the people of Beth Shemesh was that they said, "Who can stand in the presence of the LORD, this holy God?" (1 Sam. 6:20). When the earliest church was in a flood tide of revival, a Jewish couple Ananias and Sapphira lied to the Holy Spirit—and both were struck dead on the spot (Acts 5:5, 10). One might think that God's jealousy would backfire and have a reverse effect—putting off everybody. Wrong. Quite the opposite. First, "great fear seized the whole church and all who heard about these events" (v. 11). Second, it brought about an unprecedented respect by outsiders toward Christians. Although the believers had no monopoly on their place of worship at the temple, the nonbelieving Jews regarded them too highly to join them (v. 13). Third, the consequence of all this was that "more and more men and women believed in the Lord and were added to their number" (v. 14). Fourth, more power was bestowed on the church. People brought the sick into the streets and hoped that Peter's shadow might fall on some of them. "All of them were healed" (vv. 15–16).

I'm afraid that the church today, speaking generally, is ashamed of the jealousy of God. For some reason they don't want people to see this side of God's nature—as if making God look good will draw them back to the church! For a generation or more the church has worked overtime to make God look "good" and "nice." And where has it gotten us? Nowhere. The world has less respect for the church than ever. We are a pitiful sight. Things will not get better until God's ministers and people are unashamed of the true God. Like it or not, He is a jealous God. What is more, it is in our own interest that the God of Holy Scripture is *just the way He is.*

This is why He fights for us! He promises to fight for Jerusalem, and He promises to take charge of our battles in the twenty-first century. Nothing has changed. "The battle is not yours, but God's.... You will not have to fight this battle" (2 Chron. 20:15, 17). All they had to do was to sing! "Jehoshaphat appointed men to sing to the LORD...as they went out at the head of the army, saying: 'Give thanks to the LORD, for his love endures for ever.' As they began to sing and praise, the LORD set ambushes against the men of Ammon and Moab and Mount Seir who were invading Judah, and they were defeated" (vv. 21–22).

We are loved with an everlasting love (Jer. 31:3). This is why goodness and mercy follow us all the days of our lives (Ps. 23:6). It is also the reason the Holy Spirit dwells in us and "envies intensely" (James 4:5), meaning that the Spirit God caused to live in us longs jealously to give us more grace (v. 6). And He *does* give us more grace—daily. His compassions are "new every morning; great is your faithfulness" (Lam. 3:22–23).

This is amazing. Think about it. God "yearns jealously over the spirit that he has made to dwell in us," the consequence being that "he gives more grace" (James 4:5–6, ESV). This means that we are never out of His thoughts. Day and night He is focused on each of us. St. Augustine said that God loves each person as if there were no one else to love; so too He yearns jealously over each of us as if you or I were the only ones in the whole world. "How precious to me are your thoughts, O God! How vast is the sum of them! Were I to count them, they would outnumber the grains of sand. When I am awake, I am still with you" (Ps. 139:17–18).

The next time you see a grain of sand, think about this verse. Hold a handful of sand in your hand and try to count each one! Then imagine every grain of sand on the seashore. And beneath the sea. And all over the world. That is how many thoughts God has for you. Never—ever—does God take His eyes off us. When we stray from Him, His heart yearns to have us back in the fold. It is because of His jealousy. Thank God for His jealousy. It is what saves us; it is what keeps us.

As the hymn by George Matheson put it, "O love that wilt

not let me go."³ God stays with us—loving us, chastening us, watching us, guarding us, guiding us, overruling us. All because He is jealous of us. I for one am very, very glad about that. Are you?

In any case, that is the way He is. Accept this about Him. Love Him. Honor Him. Pray to Him. Worship Him. He is worthy of our worship and praise. And when we see Him one day, we will bow to Him and thank Him that our Creator God and Redeemer is *exactly like He is.*

Chapter Fourteen

GODLY JEALOUSY

As he [Jesus] approached Jerusalem and saw the city, he wept over it and said, "If you, even you, had only known on this day what would bring you peace— but now it is hidden from your eyes... because you did not recognize the time of God's coming to you."

—LUKE 19:41–44

I am jealous for you with a godly jealousy.

—2 CORINTHIANS 11:2

Moral indignation is jealousy with a halo.[1]

—H. G. WELLS

GODLY JEALOUSY IS what Jesus felt all the time. It is what Paul felt when some wicked people were beginning to lure some of his converts to a dangerous position. It is what a conscientious pastor feels toward his church members who might be tempted to do bad things. It is what Christian parents feel toward their children.

And yet this is a tricky thing. I may *think* it is godly jealousy at work in me when it may be my personal ax to grind. I *could* be so personally involved in my defense of the gospel and what I believe to be true that it is sheer jealousy rather than godly jealousy that lies behind my motivation. Yes, I could be completely "correct" and doctrinally sound in what I purport, but all I say may be nonetheless nullified by my anger in the way I say it. This disqualifies me from my claim to have godly jealousy. In a word, how I behave determines whether it is truly godly jealousy I show.

Godly jealousy is in play when you and I are angry over injustice, unrighteousness, and false teaching but are at the same time totally detached from personal rivalry, selfish motives, or vindication.

I will be as candid as I know how. I believe I have experienced godly jealousy as a Christian leader; I believe I have experienced carnal jealousy as a Christian leader. And I fear that I have experienced the latter more than the former, including (at times) in the pulpit.

In an earlier chapter I mentioned my being a pastor in Ohio. That was in 1963–1964. The church there rejected my message. I preached what they had not heard before—things like the sovereignty of God and justification by faith alone. What I preached was absolutely true. No doubt about it. But most of them weren't ready for it. About half the church signed a petition that they did not believe what I preached and that I should resign. They needed one more vote to get rid of me, but I resigned anyway.

I was young, inexperienced, and unwise. On my last Sunday I literally took my shoes off in front of the congregation and shook the dust off my feet. I would have told you then I felt like Jesus when He overthrew the moneychangers in the temple. When Jesus did that He perfectly mirrored the jealousy of God (John 2:14–17). Yes, it was godly jealousy on display when Jesus did it, but not when I did it. I was simply angry and hurt. What I did on that final Sunday in Ohio did not qualify to be called godly jealousy.

What Is Godly Jealousy?

Godly jealousy is experienced when you feel God's pain without being personally involved. This does not mean that one has no feelings in his grief. What happened to me in Ohio became personal. My ego was in the middle of it all. I should have resisted showing my personal feelings; I should have finished the final Sunday with total forgiveness—a concept (sadly) I knew little or nothing about at the time. Had I totally forgiven them for their petitions and votes against me and left with utter graciousness, I probably would have impacted them for the gospel a thousand times more than my display of shaking dust off my feet.

Godly jealousy is on display when one's personal ego is out of the picture. It is when one is devoid of an ego trip but is gripped entirely by God's feelings of jealousy.

But this is still tricky business. The heart is so deceitful and desperately wicked; who can know it? (Jer. 17:9). It is so easy to cross over a line from godly jealousy to personal finger pointing. The way some have dealt with differences or arguments over theology gives the game away. They say they are motivated by jealousy for God, but their behavior—the way they deal with brothers and sisters in Christ—suggests there may be another agenda.

The New Testament scholar F. F. Bruce has written that Paul wore his feelings on his sleeve when he wrote 2 Corinthians. This makes sense when we read this epistle. And yet Paul claimed "godly jealousy" in writing to them as he did. I do not doubt this, but I also sense that Paul was very emotionally involved when he wrote as he did.

During the course of writing this very book, I made a very pivotal theological decision. Some readers will know that a memorable series of meetings took place in Lakeland, Florida, between April and August 2008. I watched the proceedings live on GOD TV virtually every night. My first reaction was negative. Then I remembered how I initially reacted to the outpouring of the Holy Spirit at Holy Trinity Brompton in London in 1994; I was against it but later climbed down. I thought to myself as I watched the Lakeland meetings, "I cannot bear this, but I suppose I will be coming around to endorse this before long." But I never did. It had been years and years since I was so indignant in my spirit.

But was it a godly jealousy? I would like to think so. But I also know I was very angry. I knew that the gospel was not being preached. Never in my lifetime have I known such an opportunity for preaching the gospel to the *world*—and they were blowing away this opportunity. I was *so* upset. In fact, there was very little preaching at all, and when there was some exhortation, the emphasis was largely upon angels (the angel "Emma"—the supposed secret explanation for healings) and manifestations. I knew this was disgraceful. This is to say nothing about the hype, the thirty-seven claims to resurrections from the dead, and other miracles. In my regular column for a Christian magazine I put my opinion in print. In only hours after my article went to press certain revelations emerged that caused nearly everybody to suspect that the meetings were not what the supporters hoped after all. Their reasons for distancing themselves from the meetings, however, were not theological; mine were. But did I truly exhibit a godly jealousy? I can only hope.

Godly jealousy is in play when you want the gospel to be preserved. It is not your ego at stake; it is God's Word. But when you feel extremely upset, you must be very careful lest it be the flesh and not the Spirit at work.

The prophet Elijah had his finest hour on Mount Carmel. And yet he had a little bit of both—a love for the God of the Bible and an obvious ego involvement. "I am the only one of the Lord's prophets left," proclaimed Elijah (1 Kings 18:22). This was not true. First, the prophet Obadiah had taken a hundred prophets and hid them in two caves (v. 4). Second, God gently rebuked Elijah, pointing out He had "seven thousand in Israel— all whose knees have not bowed down to Baal" (1 Kings 19:18).

Elijah had a big ego and took himself very seriously. "Take my life; I am no better than my ancestors" (v. 4), but whoever said he was? It shows how driven Elijah was. Not only that, but he also added, "I have been very jealous for the LORD" (v. 14, ESV), referring to a godly jealousy—which no doubt Elijah had. But he was still very emotionally involved.

The prophet Jonah was miraculously preserved after his disobedience. He ran from God, was swallowed up by a big fish that spit him out, and was given a second chance. He forecast that judgment was coming to Nineveh. He did not stipulate conditions; he categorically prophesied that in forty days Nineveh would be destroyed by God. Lo and behold, the people of Nineveh repented—and revival came. Was Jonah pleased? No. He was keener that his prophecy be vindicated than the people of Nineveh be spared. This was the opposite of godly jealousy. The truth is, as Jeff Lucas put it, Jonah always feared what would happen "if God got out of the Israel box"! Jonah wanted any sort of revival to be exclusively Israel's privilege. Jonah resented that God would bless Nineveh. This was hardly godly jealousy.

When Paul said to his beloved Corinthians, "I am jealous for you with a godly jealousy" (2 Cor. 11:2), it was because a group of people were alienating the affection they once had for Paul to a different gospel. This group we call Judaizers—a group of Jewish people claiming to be Christians who brought the Law into the gospel in a way that undermined all that Paul taught them. They were turning Paul's very converts away from Paul, claiming that Paul did not really preach the truth to them! This was hard for Paul—extremely hard. It broke his heart that his very converts were doubting him. The issue, however, was not personal but theological. This is why Paul referred to "a Jesus other than the Jesus we preached" (v. 4).

When people preach "another Jesus" or "another gospel," it is sufficient to give the people of God a godly jealousy. But in order for it to remain *godly* jealousy one must be sure it is not his or her personal ego at stake.

Sometime ago I was preaching with my colleagues Jack Taylor and Charles Carrin. We hold "Word, Spirit, Power" conferences. But this particular church was clearly more interested in manifestations than the pure Word of God. I remember how I wrestled within as I contemplated preaching one evening. I knew that what I believe about the Word and the gospel is either true or it isn't. And if it is true, I was a coward and a complete fraud if I did not stand up to say what I knew was true. I was very nervous. My heart was pounding in my chest. I stood up and took my stand for the Word and the gospel. I spoke for eighteen minutes and (dare I say it) with as much anointing as I have had in my whole ministry. I can say I know what it is to preach with godly jealousy.

I was able to do it because it was not my pride or ego at stake at all—it was the gospel.

Jesus felt this as He wept over the city of Jerusalem. I refer to one of the most extraordinary events in Jesus's ministry. Jesus loved Jerusalem. I love Jerusalem. All Jews love Jerusalem.

I have spent time on the Mount of Olives trying to imagine precisely where it was—the very spot—Jesus was when He wept over Jerusalem. It is an amazing thing. Jesus knew who He was. He knew Jerusalem's long history. Jesus had made many trips to Jerusalem over the years—at least three a year—from Galilee. He knew what belonged to Jerusalem. He knew what was promised to Jerusalem. And yet He knew that they were about to kiss good-bye what was their own special inheritance. They were about to reject the very Messiah who was promised to them. Jesus knew He was that Messiah. It was not an ego trip for Him. It was not His pride or self-esteem; it was His love for His people and their beloved Jerusalem. "As he approached Jerusalem and saw the city, he wept over it and said, 'If you, even you, had only known on this day what would bring you peace—but now it is hidden from your eyes.... You did not recognize the time of God's coming to you" (Luke 19:41–42, 44).

He was not angry; He was brokenhearted. But it was godly jealousy.

So you don't need to feel angry to have godly jealousy. You may weep. It is the way godly parents feel when they see their beloved child getting off the straight and narrow way. You only want what is best for them. You have no desire to say "I told you so," only that you don't want them to do what is foolish.

Godly Jealousy Drives You to Share the Gospel

Paul felt godly jealousy when he was in Athens. He was waiting for Silas and Timothy to turn up and was "greatly distressed to see that the city was full of idols" (Acts 17:16). The King James Version says his "spirit was stirred"; the English Standard Version says "his spirit was provoked within him." It is what every Christian should feel today when seeing so many ads on TV that cross over a line regarding moral ethics and sexual purity, the kind of movies and entertainment available at the cinemas and theaters, the quality of education being offered, and the way godly morality is now scoffed at by top leaders in the church. It should make our blood boil. This would be godly jealousy. No ego needed here. No self-esteem. None of us trying to get elected, to get recognition, or to be honored. One is simply jealous for the righteousness that exalts a nation (Prov. 14:34).

It ought to drive us to the streets to spread the gospel. And guess what? That is *exactly* what it did to Paul; it drove Paul to take to the streets in Athens. Since he had some unexpected time on his hands while waiting for Silas and Timothy to turn up, he went to the marketplace day by day to speak "with those who happened to be there" (Acts 17:17). That is what godly jealousy led Paul to do.

Some readers will know that I invited Arthur Blessitt (the man who has carried the cross to every nation in the world) to Westminster Chapel. I was not happy when he insisted on getting us out on the streets. That is not why I asked him to preach for us. I had never done anything like that in my life. But he didn't ask me; he simply pulled me along with him. I am so glad he did. It changed my life. Our Pilot Light ministry was born. But I then went into a "low" state, wondering if what I had done was truly biblical! I worried a lot about that, especially when some of our best-known members (including some deacons) were wanting to get me fired. Then I read Acts 17:17. I found out that Paul was a Pilot Light! He went (of all places) to the marketplace and talked about Jesus Christ *with those who happened to be there.* That was what we were doing! I found my biblical warrant! And it all began because of Paul's godly jealousy.

That is not all; it led Paul to speak before the prestigious Areopagus. If Paul had marched into Athens in order to get a preaching opportunity before the Areopagus, he would have gotten as far as you or I would marching into Oxford or Cambridge hoping to address all the professors! We would be laughed to scorn. But because Paul was being faithful in the *marketplace* and wasn't even thinking about reaching the philosophers of Athens, these learned men came to him! "What is this babbler trying to say?" they asked. Paul had been preaching the good news about Jesus and the Resurrection. Then they took him to the Areopagus and asked him, "May we know what this new teaching is that you are presenting?" This was his moment. The distillation of his sermon is in Acts 17:22–31. When he finished he had three sets of people: those who sneered, those who asked him to come back, and those who were saved (vv. 32–34).

A love for the jealousy of God and the manifestation of godly jealousy will open doors for the gospel. Do not be ashamed of the jealousy of God. Instead be jealous for God. But it will be our spirit that makes the difference. I don't think Paul harangued the people in the marketplace. I think he lovingly and graciously approached people and made them want what he had. Paul's determination to know nothing but Jesus Christ and Him crucified (1 Cor. 2:2) in my opinion referred equally to two things: the content of the gospel and his being so like Jesus that the Corinthians wanted what he had.

It is like the Arab sheikh who came up to Arthur Blessitt at a Holiday Inn in Jordan and said to him, "I want what you've got." Arthur had not opened his mouth. He was merely sitting at a counter drinking a Coke. The Arab remarked it was the smile and shine on Arthur's face that made him ask to spend time with him. Arthur led him to Christ and then was introduced to dozens of sheikhs who were on business in the same hotel, whereupon Arthur preached the gospel to every one of them.

A godly jealousy is needed in the church—and in the pulpit. But what the world does not need is an angry people who show no tears, no love, and no real compassion for people's needs.

Paul had a right to speak as he did to the people in Corinth. "I promised you to one husband, to Christ, so that I might present you as a pure virgin to him"—then expressed his worry that they would be lured away from their first love and "pure devotion to Christ" (2 Cor. 11:2–3). The King James Version translates this as referring to the "simplicity" that is in Christ. Paul knew that not only might the vicious and self-righteous Judaizers succeed in turning his converts away from himself, but also that his converts would be swallowed up by deadly legalism. This is why his heart ached. His motive was not self-serving or personal; it was no ego trip. He wanted them back the way they once were—with tender hearts on fire for God.

Godly jealousy is also the cure for jealousy. Fall in love with the jealousy of God, and watch how envy and jealousy begin to dissipate in your life. Godly jealousy will bring you to aspire to the experience of John 5:44, that verse I quoted in the introduction: "How can you believe if you accept praise from one another, yet make no effort to obtain the praise that comes from the only God?" Godly jealousy will make you want the praise that comes from God only, not praise from Him plus people.

Chapter Fifteen

THIRTEEN WAYS TO
OVERCOME JEALOUSY

It is true that some preach Christ out of envy and
rivalry.... The important thing is that in every
way, whether from false motives or true, Christ is
preached. And because of this I rejoice.

—Philippians 1:15, 18

How can you believe, when you receive glory from
one another and do not seek the glory that comes
from the only God?

—John 5:44, esv

This time I will praise the Lord.

—Genesis 29:35

A T THE BEGINNING of this book I referred to three categories of jealousy: my jealousy of them, their jealousy
of me, and my making them jealous.

These three categories are closely related to each other. The
principles I shall enunciate in this chapter cover all three. Take

them seriously and apply these suggestions, and a victory over jealousy will be in your hands.

The overarching principle can be summed up: *rejoicing in the Lord*. This was Paul's own way of dealing with jealousy; it is what he recommends for the Christians at Philippi, some of whom were jealous of each other.

I doubt anybody will be as jealous of you or me as people were the apostle Paul. First, people would be naturally jealous of his pedigree. (See Philippians 3:4–6.) He was trained in the Mosaic Law by Gamaliel (Acts 22:3), the most respected teacher in ancient Judaism. At the natural level, then, nobody had a head start greater than Paul's. In addition to that, he probably had one of the greatest intellects of all time. Second, Paul became a Christian several years after the church was in existence. The disciples of Jesus were then called apostles, with James (the brother of Jesus) right in the middle of all that was going on. They were the only leaders. Then comes Saul of Tarsus, called Paul, who is like a bolt out of the blue—also claiming to be an apostle with revolutionary views about the place of the Law and the gospel—and the leaders in Jerusalem did not know how to handle him. In a word: Paul made people jealous.

When he wrote his letter to Philippi he tells how preachers in Rome were jealous of him. They preached Christ "out of envy" and even wanted to stir up trouble for him while he was in prison!

Paul's reaction: he rejoiced that—despite their motives—

Christ was preached! "Yes, and I will continue to rejoice" (Phil. 1:18).

In addition to what he was suffering while in prison, he had to do a little pastoral counseling in Philippi by remote control. Two strong women—Euodia and Syntyche—had a personal rivalry. Paul pleads with them "to agree with each other in the Lord," then says to everybody, "Rejoice in the Lord always. I will say it again: Rejoice!" (Phil. 4:2, 4).

The greatest cure for jealousy is to rejoice in the Lord and to praise the Lord.

But I will now list thirteen propositions that will bring you to victory over jealousy, whether it be your own jealousy, theirs of you, or your making them jealous.

1. Admit it to yourself.

It is true we don't want others to know we are jealous. I am not suggesting that you tell the world. But do tell it to yourself! Don't repress. Don't live in denial. Don't play games with your own heart. When someone gets your goat, admit it. When you are threatened by a friend's success, admit it. When you are not thrilled that something good happens to a friend, admit it. When you are fearful of losing what is precious to you—because of someone else's good fortune—admit it. When you fear they are brighter, better looking, abler, wiser, and more charismatic—admit it to yourself. Don't talk yourself into believing you feel other than the way you truly feel; this would not be being true to yourself. As Shakespeare said,

"To thine own self be true." If you are sad, admit it. If you are envious, admit it. If you are jealous, admit it—to yourself.

Admit it, then, when you are jealous of them—and when you know they are jealous of you. Don't repress, or don't say, "Surely they wouldn't be jealous of little old me." But what does your gut tell you? There is something about you that gets their goat, something about you that threatens them. "Do not fear what they fear" (1 Pet. 3:14). They are as insecure as you are! There is something you can do that they cannot do; there is something admirable about you that is not in them. Why is it that you don't get a warm feeling from them? It is not because you are insignificant; it is because they are threatened by your potential, your company, and the company you keep.

I have found this sometimes hard to do. I can think of several people I have tried to get close to. I have written them, phoned them, and walked up to them. I've tried so hard to be friendly. They return my friendliness either with an obvious annoyance or an ice cold plastic smile. Then it hit me. I wonder if these people are jealous of me. *Not with everybody of course.* But with some. I knew I should give up trying! Admit it: not everybody is going to like you, though not always because they are jealous of you. But sometimes that's it.

If you are causing them to be jealous, admit it. If you can't help it that they are jealous, admit it. If you are intentionally causing them to be jealous, admit it. If you are getting a buzz from making them jealous, admit it. However, this takes us to the next proposition. You should know by now that it is wrong

224

to *want* them to be jealous. When their pain gives you pleasure, you have sinned. It also means (sadly) that your jealousy toward them will give you equal pain. You will not get over your pain until you are sorry that you want to make them jealous. If making them jealous is your desire, move to the next proposition.

2. Confess it to God.

First, confess your sins. Never forget good old 1 John 1:9: "If we confess our sins, he is faithful and just and will forgive us our sins and purify us from all unrighteousness." When you have sinned by sheer jealousy, by being overcome by their jealousy of you or by your wanting to make them jealous, tell it to God. The blood of Jesus washes away all sin.

But do not do this in a perfunctory, routine sort of way. Are you sorry that you are jealous? Are you sorry that their jealousy has brought you down? Are you sorry that you delight in making them jealous? First John 1:9 is not given to us as a routine way of escape but a route by which we want to change our ways. We confess our sins because we are sorry; we confess because we want to change.

Second, confess your weakness to God. When you have confessed your sins—and are sorry but still feeling jealous, tell Him! God has big shoulders. He already knows what you are feeling. He will not be disillusioned with you. As my old friend Gerald Coates says, "He never had any illusion about us in the first place." The psalmist wrote, "You perceive my thoughts from afar" (Ps. 139:2).

"Cast your cares on the LORD and he will sustain you" (Ps. 55:22). Jesus said, "Come to me, all you who are weary and burdened, and I will give you rest" (Matt. 11:28). Peter said, "Cast all your anxiety on him because he cares for you" (1 Pet. 5:7).

The wonderful thing about telling the Lord is that He *accepts you as you are*. He doesn't laugh. He doesn't moralize. He doesn't say, "How dare you have that problem." Never. He is touched with the feeling of our weaknesses, totally and always sympathizing. After all, He Himself was tempted just as we are—and has never forgotten what it was like. That is why He still sympathizes (Heb. 2:18; 4:15).

You can even say, "I'm sorry that I'm not sorry enough." After all, one said to Jesus, "I do believe; help me overcome my unbelief!" (Mark 9:24). The apostles said to Jesus, "Increase our faith!" (Luke 17:5). God is not insecure; He can handle our transparent honesty and our slowness of progress. Confess what you feel to Him.

3. Practice total forgiveness.

This means that you totally forgive every single person who has ever hurt you and that you pray for anyone who is a threat to you. If you have not read *Total Forgiveness*, I may be asking you to do what seems out of your reach. When I was in my darkest hour and Josif Tson said, "RT, you must totally forgive them," my reaction was that I couldn't do it. But I did. And it was the best thing I ever did! So I pray that you will do it.

When you pray for those who threaten you or those who have

hurt you, you don't merely say, "Lord, I commit them to you," but you pray that God will *bless* them. I don't say it will be easy. It is like climbing Mount Everest—few do it. *But you can do it.* It is being like Jesus, who prayed, "Father, forgive them, for they do not know what they are doing" (Luke 23:34). You say, "But I'm not Jesus." True. But Stephen also did it; he prayed for the very people who killed him: "Lord, do not hold this sin against them" (Acts 7:60). It was the secret to Stephen's anointing.

Why total forgiveness? Because it is what leads you straight to *agape* love—what is described in 1 Corinthians 13. Among the descriptions of love are these words, love "does not envy" (v. 4); that is, "love never is envious nor boils over with jealousy" (AMP). Total forgiveness is the only way forward to experience this freedom from envy fully. I'm sorry, but there is no other way. Sooner or later you will have to come back to this proposition. If you succeed in applying all other suggestions, but fail in this, you will continue to struggle with jealousy—theirs and yours.

Total forgiveness also includes forgiving yourself. In *How to Forgive Ourselves—Totally*, I show how God *wants* us to forgive ourselves. The person filled with the most guilt will always be the most jealous, but when you forgive yourself, it is amazing how jealous feelings disappear. Thus when you forgive yourself—totally—you are able to love, which does not envy.

Total forgiveness even includes forgiving God. Not that God is guilty of anything wrong. Far from it! The opposite is true. He is sinless. But we nonetheless forgive God in the sense that we affirm what He chose to do for others and what He may or may not have given to us. We forgive Him if He exalts another; we forgive Him if He passes us by for the success He gave to another. "The LORD gave and the LORD has taken away; may the name of the LORD be praised" (Job 1:21). In precisely the same way, the Lord can give or withhold mercy and be just either way. We should, simply, let God be Himself.

4. Choose God's praise of you over the compliments of people.

"How can you believe if you accept praise from one another, yet make no effort to obtain the praise that comes from the only God?" (John 5:44). Never forget that this is a question our Lord put, and the implied answer is: you *cannot*. It is impossible to have faith when your priority is the praise of people. This is exactly what happened with the Jews of Jesus's day. As a result of their living for the praise of people, they were not able to believe when the Messiah turned up before their very eyes. The ultimate consequence was that jealousy set in and they missed God's visitation.

Why does John 5:44 relate to jealousy? Answer: When you live for the praise of people and are governed by what they say about you, you are inviting jealousy to walk right into your heart and take over. You will be addicted to jealousy, controlled by it. When people don't compliment you, you plummet; when they brag on you, you soar. And when others get the praise, you swallow hard, get a sickening feeling in your stomach, and get defensive. It is probably because you sought the praise of people and made no effort to obtain the kind of honor that God would have given you.

We are all guilty here. We have all done this. But John 5:44 is a magnificent way forward.

God wants to honor us. At the proper time He will exalt you (1 Pet. 5:6). And His exaltation is a thousand times greater than the trifling reward you get when you opt for the applause of people. Eye has not seen, nor ear heard, neither has it entered into anyone's mind what God has prepared for those who wait for Him. (See 1 Corinthians 2:9.)

Don't sell yourself short. God wants to bless you, exalt you, use you, encourage you, and vindicate you—far more than you want it! But you must aspire to His praise. You must want it. You must make an effort to obtain it. When *what He thinks* literally means more to you than *what they think*, watch jealousy evaporate like water in the blazing hot sun.

The cure for jealousy is to pursue God's "well done."

Question: When do you get this "well done"? Answer: two places—here below and in heaven above. That's a pretty good deal, if you ask me! God wants to bless you *now* when you set your focus on His glory; He will bless you *then* when you spend your days below making every effort to obtain the praise that comes only from Him.

Question: How do you know you have received this honor from God only? Answer: two ways—the internal witness of the Holy Spirit and the manifest blessing of God in this life. The first is the joy of the Lord. There is nothing like it here below. The second is earthly vindication. It is when God openly rewards you and makes it clear that you made the right choice. That vindication *could* even be the praise of people; God may choose to bless you by their encouragement—when it is not what you sought. But it is a blessing in life that testifies you made the right choice in living so as to make His praise your priority. It's the best way to live. And a fringe benefit of this pursuit: jealousy is kept at bay.

5. Anticipate your reward at the judgment seat of Christ.

The blessing of John 5:44 is received here below but also in heaven above. (For more details of this teaching, please see my book *Judgment Seat of Christ,* formerly called *When God Says "Well Done."*)

In a word, all who are saved will go to heaven when they die, but not all who are saved receive a reward at the judgment seat of Christ. Some will be saved by fire but lose their "reward" (1 Cor. 3:14–15)—also called "prize" (1 Cor. 9:24), "crown" (2 Tim. 4:8), and "inheritance" (Col. 3:24).

The crown is primarily hearing the Lord say well done. I know that some say, "I don't care about a prize or reward; I just want to make it to heaven." I know what they mean by that. But it is not a healthy Christian who speaks like this. Never forget that this reward was *very* important to Paul. He was not the slightest bit worried whether he would go to heaven, but he was less sure of receiving that reward: "I beat my body and make it my slave so that after I have preached to others, I myself will not be disqualified for the prize" (1 Cor. 9:27). I ask you: How will you feel when all around you take off their crowns and lay them at Jesus's feet—and you have no crown at all?

That reward will be given to those who endured persecution (Matt. 5:11–12), who blessed their enemies (Luke 6:35), who dignified their trials (James 1:12), and who eschewed the praise of people in order to obtain the sole honor of God (John 5:44).

Everybody can receive an *equal* reward as anybody else at the judgment seat of Christ. Why? Because "from everyone who has been given much, much will be demanded; and from the one who has been entrusted with much, much more will be asked" (Luke 12:48). The apostle Paul was given much more than I; therefore much more was required of him than of me. But if I am faithful in what God has entrusted me with, and Paul was faithful in what God entrusted him with, we will both receive the same reward.

So you too. Even though Paul went hungry and thirsty, was brutally treated, was homeless, was cursed (1 Cor. 4:11–12), was beaten with rods, received the thirty-nine stripes five times, was stoned, was "in danger from bandits...in the city...in the country...at sea" (2 Cor. 11:24–26), founded churches—and wrote virtually two-thirds of the books of the New Testament—you can have the same "well done" as he will get. Why? Did you have a Damascus Road vision of Jesus? Did you sit at the feet of Gamaliel? Do you have Paul's knowledge, intellect, and head start? But if you are faithful in what God has assigned to you, you have done what was required of you. Jesus said that the one who is faithful in that which is least is faithful also in much

(Luke 16:10). That means you prove how you would have done in the "much" by how you did with the "least." God requires more of some than others because they were given more to start with.

When I know that I am not required to write an epistle to the Romans because I have not been called to do so, I am set free from being jealous of the one who did. But if I am jealous that I am not Jonathan Edwards or Charles Spurgeon, I prove I do not accept my own calling; I want theirs. I am asking Peter's question, "What about him?" (John 21:21), and the Lord doesn't like that. But if I will accept my own particular calling—and be faithful in it—I will be rewarded on that day. It will be worth waiting for. But if I succumb to jealousy because I am not content with the gifts I have, I will not only be miserable all my days here on Earth but will also lose my reward at the judgment seat of Christ and be saved by fire. I don't want that.

I personally find that my greatest impetus to live a life that overcomes jealousy and is totally honoring to God is traced to the New Testament teaching on reward at the judgment seat of Christ. How we would blush in that day if it were revealed that we were governed by envy and jealousy—as unsaved people are.

Just remember: the lowest-profile person who ever lived can have a reward equal to the highest-profile person who ever lived. You can stand next to Billy Graham on that day—and have confidence (1 John 4:17)—and not feel envious of Billy. That dazzling truth alone ought to help you overcome jealousy.

6. Accept your calling.

Accepting your calling means to embrace it gladly and not look beyond it. It means to resist looking over your shoulder to see what someone else's calling is. God made you *you*. I cannot explain Einstein's theory of relativity, but I know this much: there are no two things exactly alike in the universe. Our Creator God made everything, and everything He made is unique. You are unique. Nobody is like you.

It makes God happy when you accept what He has decided what is right for you. It pleases Him when you like yourself. It is a compliment to Him that you like yourself. He made you like that. As I said in *How to Forgive Ourselves—Totally*, your heredity (parental influence) plus environment (experiences as you grew up) plus the Holy Spirit equals the way God made you. When you accept yourself as you are (with all the faults—we all have them), it makes God happy.

Never forget that your very ability, talent, hobby, interests, what comes easily, and what grips you is not of your own making. You were being prepared for such a time as this, just as Esther was (Esther 4:14). It cuts out the ground for any boasting. "Who makes you different from anyone else? What do you have that you did not receive? And if you did receive it, why do you boast as though you did not?" (1 Cor. 4:7).

Accepting your calling, then, means to affirm God's creation, His choice of parents for you, and His will when and where you should be born and how you should spend the whole of your life. He has a calling for your life—one that is infinitely better or greater than you could have come up with on your own. When you accept His will and His choice of a career—or job—you are at peace with yourself and lessen the temptation to envy or to be jealous.

7. Accept your inheritance.

This means coming to terms with the details of God's special plan for your life. It is moving from the general to the particular. For example, God's will for Israel generally was that they would inherit the land of Canaan. But He had a particular location for each tribe, and this was determined by lot. Each tribe had to accept the place where they should live. That was their inheritance. The choice was out of their hands.

So with each of us. For example, I was called to the ministry in 1954. I had no idea that in 1977 I would begin a twenty-five-year ministry at Westminster Chapel in London. That was God's idea, not mine. God has an inheritance in mind for each of us. We don't know very far in advance—if in advance at all—what that will be. As a southern gospel song puts it, we take it one day at a time.

I find Psalm 47:4 so emancipating: "He chose our inheritance for us." Wow. Think about that. It takes the pressure off us to figure it out and also to "perform." He never sets a standard we cannot reach. St Augustine prayed centuries ago, "Command what thou wilt, give what thou commandest." This means God supplies the grace it takes to obey Him. He does not command us to do something and then sit back with folded arms to see what we will do. No. He commands and then assists us to do what He told us to do. That is the way He is.

When you get your pleasure from pleasing Him, then accept His choice of inheritance. Whether it means living in London, Hong Kong, Nashville, as a doctor, lawyer, preacher, secretary, flight attendant, bus driver, office manager, postman, housewife, or nurse, you will be able to say, "The boundary lines have fallen for me in pleasant places; surely I have a delightful inheritance" (Ps. 16:6)—even if you are not called to be a king, as David was. You will recall that John the Baptist was probably tempted to be jealous that Jesus was surpassing him in popularity, and that John observed: "A man can receive only what is given him from heaven" (John 3:27).

Your inheritance is out of your hands. And so is everyone else's. This means there is no room for justified jealousy. The buck stops with God.

8. Remember that God decides what people should think of you.

God has put a ceiling on how highly people should regard you. If you try to raise that ceiling—because you think they should admire you more—you violate His purpose. What is more, you will fail. The moment you do what will cause people to esteem you more, God will step in—one way or another—to ensure that you are not admired too much. You will be admired less—I guarantee it.

This is why God sent Paul his "thorn in the flesh"—to keep him from being admired too much and also to protect Paul from himself, lest he take himself too seriously. This is why he stopped himself in saying more than he could have, lest someone would think more highly of him "than is warranted" by what he did or said (2 Cor. 12:6).

I have learned a lesson not to admire anybody too much. It never fails: every person I began to admire a little bit too much sooner or later disappointed me. Another lesson I have learned is not to let people admire me too much. It is only a matter of time that I will disappoint them.

I don't know if you have ever pondered 2 Corinthians 12:6 for very long, but if you want to overcome jealousy, let this grip you: "But I refrain [from boasting], so no one will think more of me than is warranted by what I do or say." Paul knew that God determined how highly Paul's followers should esteem him, and he was nervous about doing anything that would violate that spiritual rule. "Let another praise you, and not your own mouth; someone else, and not your own lips" (Prov. 27:2).

If God has decided what people should think of you, it follows that He has decided what people should think of others—including your friends and enemies. If people are praising and admiring your enemy, let it happen! Don't dare raise a little finger to curb their admiration of that person! If God is allowing people to think highly of that person who has done you harm, that is His sovereign business! If the world thinks highly of your enemy, leave things alone. One of the most moving episodes in the life of David was when David refused to stop Shimei from cursing him. "Leave him alone; let him curse, for the LORD has told him to. It may be that the LORD will see my distress and repay me with good for the cursing I am receiving today" (2 Sam. 16:11–12).

Don't manipulate regarding what people think of you; don't try to control what people think of your enemy. Let God handle it.

9. Let God vindicate you.

Vindication (when God clears your name) is what God does best. Don't deprive Him...don't steal from Him...don't rob Him of what He loves to do most: make you look good in His time. "It is mine to avenge; I will repay" (Deut. 32:35). Vengeance is God's prerogative and nobody else's. If you want to annoy God, try vindicating yourself! First, you won't get away with it. Second, you won't even succeed. Third, if you will take your hands off, He will do a thousand times better job of it than you would have done, even if you had years to plan it.

Consider how God vindicated Joseph. His brothers were jealous of him. Potiphar's wife falsely accused him. Who vindicated Joseph? The Pharaoh! He said before all Egypt, "There is no one so discerning and wise as you" (Gen. 41:39). Consider how God vindicated David. His brothers were jealous of him. Who vindicated David? God did it by David's killing Goliath (1 Sam. 17). Neither Joseph nor David lifted a little finger to vindicate themselves.

If God allows someone to say evil things about you or me— or things that may not be evil but simply are not true, it could be because people have begun to admire us too much and we need to be humbled. In any case, God *could* vindicate us overnight. If He withholds vindication, it is for our good! And what if we have to wait until we get to heaven to be vindicated? That is soon enough—and good enough!

When you are jealous of other people, especially if you feel they are too admired, remember that God has determined (or allowed) what people think of them and that He alone vindicates. The truth will be revealed in His time. When they are jealous of you, remember that their jealousy is one of His strange ways of preparing you for what lies ahead. If I am totally honest, the matter of jealousy has been huge in my own preparation and shaping my anointing. Their jealousy and mine has humbled me and driven me to my knees more than you will know this side of heaven.

Vindication has a way of coming along in the most unexpected way. For many years Sir Walter Scott was the leading literary figure in the British Empire. No one could write as well as he. Then the works of Lord Byron, quoted at the very beginning of this book, began to appear. Byron's greatness was immediately evident. Soon an anonymous critic praised his poems in a London paper. He declared that in the presence of these brilliant works of poetic genius, Scott could no longer be considered the leading poet of England. It was later discovered that the unnamed reviewer had been none other than Sir Walter Scott himself!

10. Develop a godly jealousy.

A godly jealousy will keep you out of a lot of trouble. For one thing, it will keep you from having personal feelings of bitterness, envy, and jealousy. But this can be tricky. Be careful here; you may think you have godly jealousy, and, before you know it, it becomes personal.

A godly jealousy is being jealous for His glory and honor. It is when it hurts you that God's name is blasphemed. It makes your heart ache when you see evil going unabated. It grieves you when pornography, sexual promiscuity, the number of abortions, the lost going to hell, and corruption in education, business, and politics continue on and on and on in an ever-increasing measure. It upsets you when the gospel is not preached. It makes you weep when heresy oozes in and out of the messages on Christian television. It saddens you when preachers appeal for money in a way that connects to people's greed.

But I repeat, we must be extremely careful here. I know what it is to feel what I sincerely believe is righteous anger—then I cross over a line, when godly jealousy becomes sheer anger. This will not do. It means I am the culprit, not them. When I am angry, I deserve judgment, not them. When I am jealous, I forfeit my right to set others straight.

How do you know it is *godly* jealousy at work? First, when your ego is not involved—even remotely. When there is an ego detachment. This would mean you have nothing to gain personally if the situation were rectified. Second, when you have no personal bitterness toward the people you are concerned about. You do not wish them anything but the blessing of God. Third, when you sincerely pray for the people in error. You don't ask God to curse them; you ask Him to bless them. You may say: "How dare I ask God to bless them when they are so wicked?" I answer: You want God to bless *them*, not what they are doing. When they feel your love for them personally, they may be convicted in a way your moralizing them will not do. Fourth, when it is truth and justice you want to prevail, not any secret enterprise of your own. Godly jealousy has eternal values in mind.

Godly jealousy, then, is not the jealousy this book has been about. Godly jealousy is a cure for jealousy.

11. Set your sight on heaven, not things of the earth.

The reason that Abraham could cope with Lot is that Abraham's focus was not on earthly affairs but on the fact that he was going to heaven. People who have heaven to live for look at earthly things in a different way. Those who have nothing to live for beyond this life must put all their eggs into one basket: the present life, money, physical and sensual pleasures, drinking and drugs, prestige, eating, owning property, and having the best of material things.

When Christians become like the world, they too want all the above—the best cars, best homes, and the best of everything that is material. You would have thought this life is all there is! You would never know they had any plans for their home in heaven! They live as though they would live here on

Earth forever! The inevitable consequence is that they battle with jealousy as much as the world.

"Set your hearts on things above, where Christ is seated at the right hand of God. Set your minds on things above, not on earthly things" (Col. 3:1–2).

> Turn your eyes upon Jesus, look full in his wonderful
>   face,
> And the things of earth will grow strangely dim
> In the light of his glory and grace.[1]
>
> —HELEN H. LEMMEL

12. Be thankful.

My friend Alan Bell reckons that you cannot be in a state of jealousy and thanksgiving at the same time. Think about that. The absence of gratitude breeds jealousy; thanksgiving kills it, if you are thankful in *everything*—as we are commanded to be. "Give thanks in all circumstances, for this is God's will for you in Christ Jesus" (1 Thess. 5:18). We are not commanded to be thankful *for* all circumstances but *in* them.

A key verse is this: "Do not be anxious about anything, but in everything, by prayer and petition, *with thanksgiving*, present your requests to God" (Phil. 4:6, emphasis added). Instead of rushing into the presence of God with your prayer list, try thanking Him for things as you ask. Start counting your blessings. If you think about it, you will find things that happened to you in the past twenty-four hours for which you are very,

very thankful—but which you took for granted. I guarantee it. Try it.

I myself had a wake-up call from the Lord over twenty years ago. He made me see how ungrateful I had been—when I had *so* much to thank Him for. I was so ashamed. I made a vow in 1986: to live the rest of my days being a very, very thankful person. I make an effort every day to thank Him for every single thing I can think of.

God loves a grateful person. It will change your life to develop a life of gratitude. Thank Him for your being alive. Thank Him for saving you. Thank Him for loving you. Thank Him for looking after you. Thank Him for His loving discipline, for the rebukes, the warnings. Thank Him for that narrow escape. Thank Him for that stranger whose word was so timely. Thank Him for the Holy Spirit, the Bible, good books, friends. Thank Him for your enemy—he or she had an important role in your development! If you take the time to recall the many ways God has blessed you, don't be surprised if you blush at the realization how little you have thanked the Lord for things.

A fringe benefit: it overcomes jealousy. Jealousy and gratitude do not coexist at the same time. Try it. Make a choice: be thankful.

13. Just praise the Lord.

"This time I will praise the LORD," said Leah after failing to win her husband's affection (Gen. 29:35). She gave up on Jacob; she turned to God and began doing the best thing a person who struggles with jealousy can do—just praise the Lord.

Praising God is the polar opposite to jealousy. It is as far from a jealous spirit as you can get. Why? Jealousy is sheer selfishness that has broken loose; praising God is the most unselfish thing you can do. Indeed, praising God is selfless, God-centered, convicting, and as devoid of self-interest as you get; it is focusing on God and not yourself.

Praising the Lord isn't easy, and it's not fun. It is boring— at first. It is much harder than thanking the Lord, because in thanking the Lord you sense you are doing something that, just maybe, will influence God to act. In other words, there is a little bit of self-interest in thanking God for things; you put your requests and petitions "with thanksgiving" (Phil. 4:6). But praise is a sacrifice. Indeed, that is what it is called: "Through Jesus, therefore, let us continually offer to God a sacrifice of praise" (Heb. 13:15).

The difference between thanking God and praising God is basically this: in thanking God you enumerate items for which you are thankful, going down a list of things He has done for *you*. Praising God is focusing on *who God is* (all-powerful, all-knowing: "his understanding has no limit"—Ps. 147:5) and what he has done *generally*—("he determines the number of the stars...sustains the humble...supplies the earth with rain"—vv. 4, 6, 8). If you want an exercise in doing nothing but praising the Lord, read the last seven psalms (Ps. 144–150). You will see exactly what praising the Lord is. Or spend time singing hymns such as "I'll Praise My Maker While I've Breath" or "Praise My Soul the King of Heaven."

There is *nothing in it for you*…except…you are honoring your Creator and Redeemer (a blessed thought) and…jealousy goes down the drain like garbage and rubbish you are so glad to get rid of. Praising the Lord is to rejoice in the Lord.

Paul's advice to a church that was struggling with unity and coping with internal jealousies, "Rejoice in the Lord always" (Phil. 4:5). After all, that is what he was doing, even though it must have hurt—a lot—to have ministers on the outside gloating that Paul was in prison. But Paul could find a silver lining in the cloud: Christ was being preached. "And because of this I rejoice. Yes, and I will continue to rejoice" (Phil. 1:18). When you look hard, you will find a cause to rejoice. And you don't have to look for a reason to praise the Lord. Just start doing it!

I like the thought that I can be a blessing to the Lord. Yes, little old me! Some modern versions of the Bible have substituted "praise the Lord" for "bless the Lord," but not all. (See the English Standard Version.) This is partly what the Bible means by the words, "Bless the Lord." This is because when you praise the Lord, you bless Him! You are a blessing to God when you praise Him. Do you like it when people are a blessing to you by saying something affirming? God likes it too. You bless Him by praising Him. This makes it all the more worthwhile!

But when you take the time to praise the Lord, you must not look over your shoulder thinking, "What will this do for me?" I can understand this, and there may be a *lot* in it for you. But don't focus on that. Charles Spurgeon once said, "I looked to Christ and the dove flew in; I looked to the dove and he disappeared." When you praise God, focus totally on Him—who He is and what He has done for humankind. Keep at it. Even if the Dove flies in—even when you are caught up in rapture—don't focus on how you feel; just keep praising the Lord. Read Psalms 144–150; sing the hymns that are God-centered.

For once, then, you and I can get our eyes off ourselves and on Him, just to praise Him for being *God*. When is the last time you did that?

Could it be that you, like Leah, have failed in your immediate goal? You pleaded and begged and God was silent. You didn't get what you wanted. Leah came into her own in an unexpected way: "I will praise the Lord" (Gen. 29:35). And yet could it be that God, as He was with Leah, has been angling to get your attention all this time? For one reason: to let Him have the last word.

Our time together has come to an end. Let this warning never leave you: jealousy will ruin your life. Let this truth reverberate in your heart. God loves you so much. He is jealous for you. Turn your back on your own jealousy.

Thank God for His.

NOTES

Foreword

1. HP-Time and Gerald Clarke, "Show Business: New Notes From an Old Cello," *TIME*, August 15, 1983, http://www.time.com/time/magazine/article/0,9171,949754-3,00.html (accessed January 26, 2010).

2. William Shakespeare, *As You Like It*, 5.2. References are to act and scene, as viewed at http://shakespeare.mit.edu/asyoulikeit/full.html (accessed January 26, 2010).

Introduction
Coping With Jealousy

1. William Shakespeare, *Othello* 3.3.189–190. Refererences are to act, scene, and line, as viewed at http://www.shakespeare-online.com/plays/othello_3_3.html (accessed September 4, 2009).

2. ThinkExist.com, "Lord Byron Quotes," http://thinkexist.com/quotation/yet_he_was_jealous-though_he_did_not_show_it-for/198352.html (accessed July 16, 2009).

3. ThinkExist.com, "Gore Vidal Quotes," http://thinkexist.com/quotation/whenever_a_friend_succeeds_a_little_something_in/10930.html (accessed July 16, 2009).

4. Martha Tarbell, *Teachers' Guide to International Sunday School Lessons for 1912* (New York: Fleming H. Revell, 1911), 440; viewed at http://books.google.com/books?id=yogBAAAAYAAJ&source=gbs_navlinks_s (accessed September 4, 2009).

5. "Rock of Ages" by Augustus Toplady. Public domain.

Chapter 2
Gospel Jealousy

1. "Jesus Thy Blood and Righteousness" by Nikolaus L. von Zinzendorf, translated by John Wesley. Public domain.

2. This article can be viewed in the archives of several newspapers, including: David Haldane, "U.S. Muslims and Mormons Share Deepening Ties," *Los Angeles Times*, April 2, 2008, http://articles.latimes.com/2008/apr/02/local/me-morlims2 (accessed September 14, 2009).

3. "My Hope Is Built" by Edward Mote. Public domain.

4. "A Safe Stronghold Our God Is Still" by Martin Luther, translated by Thomas Carlyle. Public domain.

Chapter 3
Racial and National Jealousy

1. Nancy Samalin, *Loving Your Child Is Not Enough* (New York: Penguin, 1998), 151.

Chapter 4
Motivational Jealousy

1. "God Moves in a Mysterious Way" by William Cowper. Public domain.

Chapter 7
Ridiculing Jealousy

1. ThinkExist.com, "Lawrence Durrell Quotes," http://thinkexist.com/quotation/it_is_not_love_that_is_blind-but_jealousy/214590.html (accessed July 29, 2009).

Chapter 8
Perilous Jealousy

1. ThinkExist.com, "John Milton Quotes," http://thinkexist.com/quotes/john_milton/ (accessed July 29, 2009).

Chapter 10
Fatal Jealousy

1. WorldofQuotes.com, "Hannah More Quotes," http://www.worldofquotes.com/author/Hannah-More/1/index.html (accessed September 29, 2009).

CHAPTER 13
THE JEALOUSY OF GOD

1. Oprah.com, "A New Earth Online Class," chapter 1 transcript, as viewed at CraigDayton.com, http://www.craigdayton.com/craigdayton/pdf/transcript01.pdf (accessed October 1, 2009).

2. Ibid.

3. "O Love That Wilt Not Let Me Go" by George Matheson. Public domain.

CHAPTER 14
GODLY JEALOUSY

1. H. G. Wells, *The Wife of Sir Isaac Harman* (n.p.: BiblioLife, 2008), 299.

CHAPTER 15
THIRTEEN WAYS TO OVERCOME JEALOUSY

1. "Turn Your Eyes Upon Jesus" by Helen H. Lemmel. Public domain.